a closet full of
SHOES

a closet full of
SHOES

Simple Ways to Make Them Chic

Jo Packham
Sara Toliver

Chapelle, Ltd.
P.O. Box 9252, Ogden, UT 84409
(801) 621-2777 • (801) 621-2788 Fax
e-mail: chapelle@chapelleltd.com
Web site: www.chapelleltd.com

Library of Congress Cataloging-in-Publication Data

Packham, Jo.
   A closet full of shoes : : simple ways to make them chic / Jo Packham & Sara Toliver.
      p. cm.
   "A Sterling/Chapelle book."
   Includes index.
   ISBN-13: 978-1-4027-2426-8
   ISBN-10: 1-4027-2426-8
   1.   Shoes.   2.   Fancy work.   I. Toliver, Sara. II. Title.

TT678.5.P33 2006
685'.31--dc22
                                                            2005026940

10 9 8 7 6 5 4 3 2 1
Published by Sterling Publishing Co., Inc.
387 Park Avenue South, New York, NY 10016
©2006 by Jo Packham and Sara Toliver
Distributed in Canada by Sterling Publishing
c/o Canadian Manda Group, 165 Dufferin Street
Toronto, Ontario, Canada M6K 3H6
Distributed in the United Kingdom by GMC Distribution Services,
Castle Place, 166 High Street, Lewes, East Sussex, England BN7 1XU
Distributed in Australia by Capricorn Link (Australia) Pty. Ltd.
P.O. Box 704, Windsor, NSW 2756, Australia
Printed and Bound in China
All Rights Reserved

Sterling ISBN-13: 978-1-4027-2426-8
         ISBN-10: 1-4027-2426-8

Table of Contents

8   Introduction

10   Tips and Ideas for Decorating Shoes

16   Put Your Feet Up:
Shoes for the Spa and Beach

32   Stepping Out:
Evening and Party Shoes

52   Walking Down the Aisle:
Shoes for Brides and Bridesmaids

64   Running Around:
Everyday Shoes

84   Walking Tall: Boots

94   Baby Steps: Shoes for Little Ones

106 Fancy Footwork

135 Patterns

138 Acknowledgments

143 Metric Equivalency Charts

144 Index

Introduction

As character Carrie Bradshaw once put it on an episode of "Sex and the City," "It's really hard to walk in a single woman's shoes—that's why you sometimes need really special shoes!"

Single or not, women love a really great pair of shoes. There's something about sexy stiletto heels, funky platforms, or breezy flip-flops that lightens our moods and puts a spring in our steps. We can justify owning multiple pairs up to a point—boots for winter, sandals for summer, a pair of brown shoes, a pair of black—but after that it's purely shoe-lust that drives us to purchase those bold, brazen, completely impractical forms of footwear that we love so much.

Wearing a great pair of shoes directly from the department store is one thing, but wearing shoes that you've decorated yourself is something else. Embellished shoes stand out from the rest, whether they're just a bit different or completely decked out and begging to be flaunted. Just knowing that you have a pair unlike any other in the world is rewarding in itself.

Embellishing adds that extra something—the sparkle of glittery beads, the shine of jewels, the femininity of flowers, the texture of ribbon. It breathes new life into old shoes, adds pizzazz to boring shoes, and creates beauty where none existed. You can take an old, forgotten pair from the back of your closet or a gently worn flea-market find and make it look and feel completely new. Plus, you can easily make a bag or hat to match by simply using the same materials.

This book will show you that for just pennies, you can give any kind of shoe—whether sandals, sneakers, or stilettos—an expensive designer look. The first two pages of each chapter contain shoes with simple embellishments to show how quickly and easily you can create a chic look. We've even included some purchased shoes along with the embellished ones for comparison—and we bet you won't be able to tell the difference. The rest of the projects are more detailed and take more time, and are all the more rewarding when you slip them on and show them off.

Our obsession with shoes has gone beyond the world of apparel as well. These days, shoes can be works of art. Leaf through our gallery section and you will find some very imaginative shoes that are more at home on a pedestal than a foot.

So jump in with both feet! Let that shoe-lust take over and start creating all kinds of unique shoes. Put your own spin on them—you'll have lots of fun along the way, and better yet, you'll end up with "really special" shoes that are completely your own.

Tips and Ideas for Decorating Shoes

Chances are, you're not going to find the same pair of shoes and the same colors and styles of ribbons, jewels, etc., that we have used in this book. So let the instructions guide you in design techniques as you personalize the pair in the colors, textures, and trinkets that appeal to you.

The best part is that you can spend very little to get a designer look. Start with an old pair from your closet that doesn't match anything, and paint it or cover it with fabric. Thrift-store shoes that are in good condition but happen to be hideous can be turned into treasures with some creativity. Spend a few bucks on plain canvas shoes or flip-flops at the discount store and have fun creating different looks.

Once you get going, you can really branch out and create your own designs. Let these general ideas and tips guide you through the endless possibilities.

Silk Flowers

Silk flowers add color and femininity to shoes. They are perfect for strappy summer sandals and flip-flops. Purchase sprays of silk flowers in colors that coordinate with your shoes. Use one or two large blossoms or several small ones per shoe. Cut them close to the stem with wire cutters and adhere to the shoe with industrial-strength adhesive for plastic or leather shoes, or hot glue for fabric shoes.

Ribbons and Trim

Use your imagination to create all kinds of looks with decorative trims and pretty ribbons. Use the structure of the shoe to dictate where to apply. Adhere them along the sides and straps of flip-flops, across toe straps of sandals, around the instep of a slip-on flat, or across the toe of a mule.

With fabric shoes, you can use strong double-sided adhesive sheets, hot glue, fabric adhesive, or needle and thread to secure the ribbon or trim. Industrial-strength adhesive will create a strong bond to plastic or leather.

Designer Tip:

Industrial-strength adhesive is one of the best adhesives for gluing materials to shoes. It adheres to many surfaces and forms an extremely strong bond that will stand up to the wear and tear shoes go through. Just make sure you're in a well-ventilated area when working with it, and that you let the glue dry for 24 hours before wearing the shoes.

Paint

Paint gives you endless possibilities when it comes to color and design. You can paint motifs like flowers, fruit, animals, or anything else you can think of. The trick is to practice drawing your design on paper several times before drawing it onto the shoe. Once you have determined your pattern or image, draw it onto the shoe with a pen or pencil, then fill in as desired with paint.

Paint can also be used for geometric designs like stripes, diamonds, or polka dots. A round object dipped in paint, like a pencil eraser, creates perfect circles. You can use low-tack masking tape or blue painter's tape to mask off stripes. Of course, you can always draw designs freehand.

Fabric shoes are perfect candidates for paint because they absorb it so well. Acrylic paints are suitable for this. Other types of materials must be primed before they are painted with acrylics. For plastic shoes, it is helpful to go over areas that will be painted with sandpaper. You can also use plastic paint on these surfaces.

For leather and patent leather shoes, acetone will strip shiny finishes so that the paint will adhere better. Apply it with a cotton ball on just the areas that will be painted. If not using acetone, make sure to remove all dirt and oils with alcohol before you begin painting. Another option is to sand the surface of leather and patent leather shoes if necessary. A rough surface will also absorb paint better.

Jewelry

Attaching pins, brooches, and clip-on earrings is a simple way to add glam and panache to evening shoes. Look for unusual vintage pieces at thrift stores and flea markets. You can often find inexpensive costume jewelry at department stores.

Attach jewelry pieces to the heel or to the toe at the instep, or pin them onto a strap. Just make sure the pin or clip doesn't irritate your foot. If it does, cut it off with wire cutters. You can then adhere the piece to the shoe with tape for a temporary bond or industrial-strength adhesive for a permanent bond.

Appliqué

Iron-on appliqués are perfect for adorning fabric shoes. Appliqués can be applied to any fabric with a smooth finish, excluding nylon. Keep an eye out for pretty patterns and designs that would fit on the toe or sides of shoes, in appealing complementary colors. Then simply follow the product instructions for adhering to the shoes.

"I did not have three thousand pairs of shoes. I had one thousand and sixty."
—Imelda Marcos

Beads and Buttons

Beads and buttons are natural embellishments for shoes. Whether you use dozens of little ones to cover the entire surface or a single large one on the toe, they add sparkle, texture, and color to shoes. Use the structure of the shoe to dictate placement—along seams, across toe straps, etc. Flat beads are good bets; their large surface area will adhere to shoes better. An industrial-strength adhesive will create an extremely strong bond.

Fused-glass beads are wonderful for their beauty and color. If you are familiar with cutting and firing glass, the following instructions will help you create prismatic glass beads. Experiment with different sizes, shapes, and colors.

If you would rather purchase beads, dichroic glass beads and fused Italian millefiori disks are generally available at bead stores or online. Experiment and have fun mixing and matching colors when applying the beads to the shoes. Both shoes don't have to be identical.

Glass Beads

Alcohol	Glass cutter
Clean rag	Kiln
Clear fusible glass	Ruler
Dichroic fusible glass	Superglue

1. Cut two rectangles of clear fusible glass to approximately 3" x 4". Cut one rectangle of fusible dichroic glass to 3" x 4". Using the rag, clean all glass with alcohol.

2. Stack the pieces of glass, sandwiching the dichroic glass between the clear pieces. Drop a small dot of superglue on each corner, adhering all three layers together.

3. Place glass on prepared surface in kiln. Fuse to 1450°F, using the firing schedule for the kiln. After the kiln reaches room temperature, take the glass out and clean with alcohol again.

4. On the back of the glass, draw a grid of ¼"–½" squares. Using a glass cutter, cut along the lines.

5. Repeat Step 3 to re-fuse the glass. The pieces will become rounded, smooth-edged, and dome-shaped to form beads.

Put Your Feet Up:
Shoes for the Spa
and the Beach

Sometimes your feet need a vacation just as much as the rest of your body does. When you're at the spa or the beach or even just at home, treat your feet to casual flip-flops, easy slides, or soft slippers.

Top Dog Sneakers

These darling sneakers put your favorite pet's face on display. This project uses black paint to match the dog's fur, but you can use colors to suit your pet.

Accessories

1¹/₂" headpins (6)

Alphabet beads

Computer, paper, printer, and scanner (optional)

Craft scissors

Fabric adhesive

Fabric paint

Multihole brackets (2) or split rings (6)

Pair of children's white sneakers

Paw print rubber stamp (optional)

Photo of favorite pet

Photocopier

Pliers

Small paintbrush

1. Using the small paintbrush and fabric paint, create racing stripes down the sides of the sneakers. Let dry.

2. Paint or stamp several paw prints along only the middle and back of the sneakers. Let dry.

3. Photocopy a photo of the pet's face at a copy center, or scan and print it onto printer paper.

4. Crop the printed photo. Using the fabric adhesive, glue onto the front of the sneakers.

5. Using the alphabet beads, spell out pet's name. String the first set of name beads onto a headpin and, using pliers, create a small loop at the end. Repeat on remaining shoe.

6. Use the four remaining headpins to either spell out other words or use decorative beads and use the same loop-making technique to create the rest of the bead dangles for the sneakers. There are two ways to attach the bead dangles to the shoelaces:

a. If you have a multihole bracket that slides over the laces (like the one in this project), slip the loop you created at the tip of each headpin through one of the holes in the bracket. Then squeeze the headpin's loop closed so it is secure as it dangles off the bracket.

b. If you don't have brackets, use the same method to attach each headpin to one of the split rings. String the split rings onto the laces and lace up the sneakers.

Designer Tip:

Another option when adhering photos to fabric shoes is to create an iron-on transfer. To do this, you need a computer, photo-imaging software, a printer, and transfer paper. Download or scan the photo into the computer, then flip it to a mirror image using the photo-imaging software. Print onto printer paper first to make sure it looks right, then print the image onto transfer paper. You will then need to iron it onto white cotton fabric before adhering to the shoe.

You can also use transfer software, which should lead you through the process step by step. The software is available online or at computer/electronics stores. Transfer paper is usually available at crafts stores.

Woven Ribbon Flip-flops

Tapestry or woven ribbon adds a stylish texture to a pair of flip-flops.

Accessories

2"-wide tapestry/woven ribbon (1 yard)
Fabric scissors
Industrial-strength adhesive
Pair of flip-flops
Pins

1. Determine amount of ribbon needed by placing ribbon on the flip-flop straps and simulating the desired ripples and wrinkles. Cut a length from ribbon for each shoe to the determined measurement.

2. Tie a knot on both ends of the ribbon. Trim the ends that protrude from the knots. Cut the ribbon into two equal lengths.

3. Apply glue along one strap. Starting at the outside of the shoe, adhere the ribbon to the strap, beginning with the knotted end. Press the ribbon into the glue, creating wrinkles and ripples as you go. Secure as needed with pins.

4. When you reach the center post, wrap the ribbon around the post and up to the front of the post again. Trim off the excess ribbon and tuck the trimmed end under the wrap you just made.

5. Apply glue along the remaining strap. Adhere the ribbon as in Step 3.

6. When you reach the center post, wrap the end of the ribbon around the post loosely a few times to create the look of a full knot. Apply glue to the end and tuck it under. Secure with pins until dry.

7. Repeat Steps 2–6 with the remaining flip-flop.

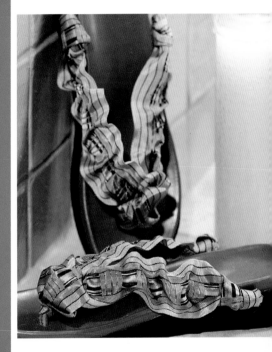

"I'm not at home, but my shoes are. Leave them a message."
—Sex and the City

21

Beach Stompers

These high-top canvas sneakers use five different colors of paint. Use whatever designs and colors you desire; just make sure they are colors that will show up on the canvas.

Accessories

Acrylic paints in desired colors
Drinking glass
Foam stamps
Heavy sewing thread or light fishing line
Large-eyed needle
Newspaper
Paintbrush
Pair of canvas high-top sneakers
Rubber band
Thrift shop necklace, disassembled

1. Stuff toe of shoe with newspaper to make firm.

2. Place drinking glass in ankle portion and hold upright with rubber band.

3. Using brush, apply acrylic paint to the stamp, making sure to avoid getting any paint on the edges.

4. Press stamp firmly on fabric of shoe. Use fingers to press from behind if any portion of fabric doesn't make direct contact. Let paint dry.

5. Stitch on beads from necklace with thread or fishing line. *Note: Sneakers shown were embellished with a shell necklace.*

6. Repeat Steps 1–5 with remaining shoe.

Rhinestone Sneakers

These shoes are simple because they are decorated only at the toe. Our sneakers came with a rubber toe. If your shoes have a fabric toe, simply use industrial-strength adhesive to glue the rhinestones to the fabric.

Accessories

Craft scissors

Pair of canvas slip-on shoes

Rhinestones

Tweezers

1. Cut two pieces from the adhesive sheet to fit the toe area of each shoe.

2. Remove one side of the adhesive sheet and apply firmly to the toe of one shoe, smoothing out any wrinkles.

3. Remove the remaining side of the adhesive. Using tweezers, apply the rhinestones in an orderly manner to ensure that gaps are minimal. Press the stones down as firmly as possible.

4. Repeat Steps 2–3 with remaining shoe.

Polka Dot Flip-flops

A handmade ribbon "pom-pom" decorates the toe of these cute sandals.

Accessories

¼"-wide ribbon

⅜"-wide polka-dot ribbon

Fabric scissors

Heavy-duty thread

Hot-glue gun and glue sticks

Large buttons (4)

Pair of flip-flops

1. Place ribbon around the sides of one flip-flop to determine amount needed. Cut two lengths from ribbon for each shoe to the determined measurement.

2. Beginning at back center, hot-glue one length of ribbon around the top edge of the side. Hot-glue remaining length of ribbon along the bottom edge of side.

3. Glue button on back where beginning and end of ribbon lengths meet.

4. Thread the heavy-duty thread through the remaining button and tie the thread in a knot. Make the ribbon pom-pom by looping ¼"-wide ribbon into several 2½"-diameter loops. Using the ends of the button thread, tie a knot around center of the ribbon loops.

5. Cut another length from ¼"-wide ribbon to 6". Tie the ribbon in a knot around the top of the toe post. Thread each end of the knot through a loop on either side of the ribbon pom-pom and tie the ends into a knot twice to secure pom-pom to the toe.

6. Repeat Steps 2–5 with the remaining flip-flop.

Berry Terry Flip-flops

Soft white terry-cloth slippers adorned in berries create a chic soothing spa style.

Accessories

Adhesive dots
Berry sprays (2)
Hot-glue gun and glue sticks
Pair of white terry-cloth flip-flops
Ribbon to match color of berries (2 yards)
Wire cutters

1. Using wire cutters, cut the berry sprays into sprigs and single berries.

2. Hot-glue the berries onto the center of the top of the sandal.

3. Complete the look with leaves and more berries, making sure to cover up stems.

4. Repeat Steps 2–3 with remaining shoe.

Beaded Fringe Flip-flops

Long beads dangle from the straps of these chic shoes. We used two layers of trim on each flip-flop because the beads were so far apart. If the beads on your trim are closer together, you can use just one layer.

Accessories

Hot-glue gun and glue sticks

Pair of fabric flip-flops

Pins

Trim with long beaded fringe ($\frac{1}{2}$ yard)

1. Lay trim along straps to determine amount needed. Cut two lengths from the trim for each shoe to determined measurement.

2. Hot-glue one length of trim along the straps of the flip-flop from one end to the other. Hot-glue remaining length on top, staggering the beads. Trim any excess. *Note: If beads are coming apart at the trim ends, secure them with hot-glue.* Secure with pins until dry. Repeat with remaining flip-flop.

French Knot Slippers

These cashmere slippers are adorned in French Knots and crocheted trim. Make sure the fabric weave of your slippers is open enough to accept the crochet hook head.

Accessories

Confetti yarn

Craft scissors

Craft thread in
   desired colors (4)

Large-eyed needle

Small crochet hook

1. Double crochet a band of yarn along the instep. Double crochet another band of yarn just above the first band. *Note: if you do not know how to crochet, you can sew small lace trim to the instep.*

2. Begin making French Knots with one color of craft thread. Make sure thread is long enough to do entire top of slipper. Start thread as close to the edge of the slipper as possible so as to not rub foot with knots. Move from one side to the other and tie off close to sole. Repeat with remaining colors until slipper toe is covered as desired.

3. Repeat Steps 1–2 with remaining slipper.

Luxe Quilted Slippers

You will feel like a queen in these plush, gilded slippers.

Accessories

Large gold buttons (2)
Needle and matching thread
Scissors
Small gold beads

1. Stitch large buttons onto the center top of each slipper.

2. Stitch the gold beads from the inside, onto the top of slippers at each corner of the quilting.

"It's easier to put on slippers than to carpet the whole world."

—Al Franken

Girly Decoupage Shoes

Pick a fabric with motifs in any theme for these shoes. Here, we used a pretty, "girly" fabric with motifs of lipstick, nail polish, and perfume.

Accessories

½" paintbrush

¾" paintbrush

Acrylic paint

Alcohol

Black fine-line permanent marker

Cotton balls

Disposable paintbrush

Fabric scissors

Fabric with motif pattern

Industrial-strength adhesive

Leather shoes

Pencil

Plastic paint primer

Plastic paint sealer

Ruler

1. Using a cotton ball, clean shoes with alcohol.

2. Using ¾" paintbrush, paint two coats of plastic paint primer over surface of shoes, allowing 15 minutes of drying time between coats. Rinse paintbrush. Allow 30 minutes to one hour before applying paint.

3. Using pencil and ruler, lightly draw vertical lines onto the shoes.

4. Using the ½" paintbrush, paint in the lines with acrylic paint.

5. While paint dries, cut out desired motifs from the fabric.

6. Using industrial-strength adhesive and disposable paintbrush, glue images onto shoes. Make sure the back side of the entire image is covered. *Note: Try to keep the images still, as moving them around will remove paint and leave glue marks.*

7. Use the marker to draw decorative lines around the decoupage images. Let marker dry.

8. Paint both shoes with two coats of plastic paint sealer, allowing 45 minutes of drying time between coats.

Designer Tip:

When applying liquids like paint or primer to shoes, it is helpful to place the shoe on a piece of paper so that you can rotate the shoe without touching it.

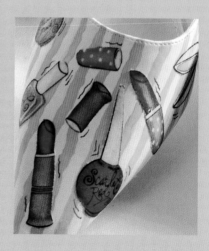

Put on your dancing shoes!

Stepping Out:
Evening and Party Shoes

*Eveningwear requires some ostentation —
the glint of jewels, the drama of silk
and velvet, the brazen colors and frills of
flowers. Strap on the flashy sandals
and heels in this chapter, and your
feet will feel like dancing.*

"Give a girl the correct footwear and she can conquer the world."

—Bette Midler

Peacock Mules

You'll be proud to "strut your stuff" in these eye-catching heels and a matching bag. A clever painting technique creates a completely unique pattern.

Accessories

³/₄" paintbrush
Acetone
Cotton balls
Hair dryer
Liquid starch (1 quart)
Pair of turquoise mules
Paper towel
Peacock feathers
Plastic paint primer
Plastic paint sealer
Plastic paints in black, bright blue, and apple green
Shallow container such as a 10" x 13" baking pan
Superglue
Water
Wide-tooth comb

1. Rub area of shoes that will be painted with a cotton ball dipped in acetone.

2. Paint two thin coats of plastic paint primer on shoes, using ³/₄" paintbrush, allowing 15 minutes of drying time between coats. Rinse brush. Allow 30 minutes to one hour before applying paint.

3. Tape off any areas of shoes you do not want painted.

4. Thin the plastic paints with water.

5. Pour liquid starch into a shallow container until at least 1" deep. Drizzle all three paints onto the starch. Using comb, gently swirl paint.

6. Dip shoes into mixture, one side at a time, wiping up drips from bottom of shoe. Immediately use the blow dryer to dry the paint before too much drips off.

7. Once dry, carefully use a wet paper towel to clean off any dripped paint from around soles and bottoms of shoes.

8. Paint shoes with two coats of plastic paint sealer, allowing 45 minutes dry time between coats.

9. Glue peacock feathers in desired areas.

Exotic Asian Heels

Iron-on appliqué is a wonderful way to adorn shoes. Just make sure the appliqué is small enough to fit onto the shoe.

Accessories

Iron-on appliqués
Pair of fabric high heels
Small-tipped craft iron

1. Determine placement of the appliqués on the shoes.

2. Following the instructions that accompany the appliqués, carefully iron into place.

Braided Rope Mules

The satin sheen of braided rope trim creates an elegant look when paired with faux pearls.

Accessories

26-gauge wire

Black acrylic paint

Braided rope trim

Fabric scissors

Faux pearls

Hot-glue gun and
  glue sticks

Paintbrush

Pair of mules

1. Place trim around instep to determine amount needed. Cut a length from trim for each shoe to determined size.

2. Wrap ends of both lengths of trim with wire to prevent fraying. Paint the ends with shoe color so that they are camouflaged against the shoe.

3. Hot-glue trim around instep of one shoe.

4. Coil a length of trim and hot-glue to the center of the toe. Tuck in the ends of the coil and hot-glue underneath to secure.

5. Hot-glue pearls as desired onto the trim.

6. Repeat Steps 3–5 with remaining shoe.

Flashy Foil Strappies

Try this mosaic technique for adding pizzazz to humdrum evening shoes.

Accessories

12" sheet of aluminum foil
Black posterboard
Craft scissors or rotary cutter and grid
Decoupage medium
Lacquer
Pair of black fabric high heels
Spray adhesive
Tacky craft glue

1. Using spray adhesive, adhere the dull side of the aluminum foil sheet to a piece of black posterboard. *Note: This thickens the papers and makes them easier to cut and work with. It also gives the papers dimension so that the final project will resemble mosaic.*

2. Cut aluminum foil sheet into squares. *Note: The size of the squares should depend on the amount of time you want to spend completing the project. These shoes are done in ¼" squares, but ½" squares will work, too.*

3. Glue the tiles onto one shoe. Place the tiles in vertical and horizontal lines, trimming them as necessary before gluing them down. *Note: Paper tends to curl and move around a bit until the glue sets. If papers lift, gently press them back into place until they stay down.*

4. When the glue is completely dry, cover the entire shoe in a thick coat of decoupage medium. Let dry.

5. Spray two coats of the lacquer on the entire shoe. Let dry.

6. Repeat Steps 3–5 with remaining shoe.

Designer Tip:

Choose a pair of black fabric high heels for this project. The black is a nice contrast to the foil and the fabric is a porous surface that absorbs the glue and holds the paper tiles in place. Leather is not a good choice for this project because it may not absorb enough glue to hold the tiles in place.

Blossom Sandals
and Hat

Create a garden at your toes with bunches of silk blossoms.

Accessories

Brightly colored flowers (2 bunches)
Hot-glue gun and glue sticks
Matching hat
Pair of high-heeled sandals
Wire cutters

1. Cut blossoms from the flower bunches.

2. Divide the blossoms evenly between the two shoes so that they will receive the same coverage. Hot-glue the flowers onto the toe straps, covering them completely.

3. Hot-glue leftover flowers onto one side of the hat along the brim.

Grapevine Sling-backs

Slip on these sling-backs, and you'll be dreaming of Napa vineyards and leisurely sips of pinot noir on the patio.

Accessories

Craft scissors
Glass grape bunches (2)
Hot-glue gun and glue sticks
Needle and invisible thread
Pair of sling-backs

1. Cut a grape bunch into small clusters. Position the clusters across the toe strap in desired arrangement.

2. Stitch grape stem to the toe strap. Hot-glue grapes to each other to secure them more permanently.

3. Hot-glue the leaves and additional individual grapes to complete the look. Make sure to glue the grapes and leaves to the stitched-on grape bunch only. *Note: This allows you to remove the decorations easily without damaging the shoe, so that you can wear the shoes without the grapes when desired.*

4. Repeat Steps 1–3 with remaining shoe.

Feathered Mules

Chic plumage adorns this simple pair of mules.

Accessories

Bag of feathers
Craft scissors
Glue
Matching trim
Pair of mules

1. Divide the feathers evenly between the two shoes. Choose feathers that are well shaped and are graduated in length. Strip off the downy part of each feather and trim the feather so that it is not too long.

2. Determine the placement of feathers. Glue the longest feather onto the center of the toe of one shoe. Move down the shoe on both sides, adding feathers as you go. *Note: You can extend the shaft of the feather beyond the toe into the center of the shoe. Once the glue is dried the ends will be trimmed off.*

3. Trim the ends of the feathers that extend into the shoe bed so that they do not show or cause irritation.

4. Glue trim over the trimmed feather area. Tuck each end under the instep for a neat finish.

5. Repeat Steps 2–4 with remaining shoe.

Jeweled Ballet Slippers

If you ever dreamed of owning a pair of ballet slippers as a girl, these pretty gem-adorned shoes are for you.

Accessories

¼"-diameter silver rings (20)
Hot-glue gun and glue sticks
Pair of black ballet slippers
Rhinestones in a variety of colors and shapes
Sheer black ribbon (2 yards), cut in four
   equal lengths

1. Thread the silver rings onto two lengths of sheer black ribbon. Hot-glue the ribbon to the instep edge of one shoe in loops. Tie the ends of each ribbon to the elastic on either side of the shoe.

2. Hot-glue the rhinestones around the edge of the instep in a random manner. Remove any glue "strings" and excess glue.

3. Repeat Steps 1–2 with remaining shoe.

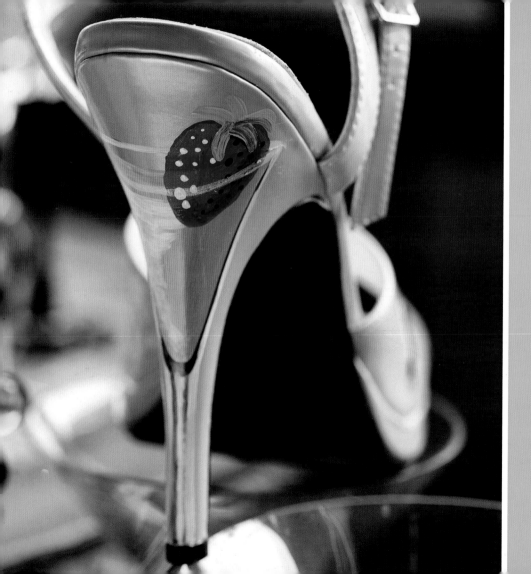

Martini Party Shoes

Bring out your "inner party girl" with a pair of whimsical cocktail-motif sandals.

Accessories

Alcohol

Bag of feathers

Cotton balls

Craft scissors

Glue

Pair of sling-backs

Thin black trim

1. Use a cotton ball to clean the shoes with alcohol.

2. Paint two coats of plastic paint primer over shoes, allowing 15 minutes of drying time between coats. Allow 30 minutes to one hour before applying paint.

3. Using a pencil, draw or trace the Martini Party Shoes patterns on page on 135 onto shoes as desired.

4. Thin the plastic paint with water. Paint in the designs. *Note: It may take two to three coats to get the desired coverage.*

5. Once completely dry, paint shoes with two coats of plastic paint sealer, allowing 45 minutes of drying time between coats.

Here's to world peace and cute shoes!

Harlequin Jester Shoes

These shoes are begging to party, whether at a birthday bash or a masquerade ball.

Accessories

20-gauge wire

Acetone

Black acrylic paint

Cotton balls

Craft knife

Fine gold glitter

Flowers

Glossy spray urethane

Industrial-strength adhesive

Paintbrushes

Pair of purple leather high heels

Pen

Ribbons in various styles and colors,
   including velvet

Star jewels

Superglue

Wired pearls

1. Rub shoes with a cotton ball dipped in acetone.

2. Paint the outside half of each shoe with black. Let paint dry.

3. Trace Harlequin Shoes pattern on page 136 over the entire surface of each shoe with the pen.

4. Paint in every other harlequin with black on the purple side of each shoe. Let paint dry.

5. On the black side of one shoe, carefully apply superglue onto one harlequin at a time, then sprinkle with glitter. *Note: Make sure the glitter harlequins mirror the purple harlequins on the opposite side of the shoe.* Repeat this process in every other harlequin. Let glue dry. Repeat with remaining shoe.

6. Clean off excess glitter from shoes. Spray shoes with urethane. Let dry.

7. Near the top of the heel of one shoe, cut approximately ½" slit lengthwise on either side of the seam with craft knife. Thread velvet ribbon through both slits to the inside of the shoe and pull through until ribbon length is even on both sides. *Note: This ribbon will be used to tie up the ankle.*

8. To make the ribbons that top off the heel, lay down an 18" length of wire. Center the ribbon at the bottom of the wire, then wrap wire around ribbon a few times. Repeat down the length of wire with remaining ribbons until you have a cluster of ribbons, leaving a few inches of wire at the end. Trim the ends as desired.

9. Thread the wire end under the velvet ribbon on the back of the heel. Wrap the wire around a few times to secure ribbon cluster to heel.

10. Cut a small horizontal slit at toe near the edge of the instep. Wrap wire around the center of a bunch of wired pearls and twist it together. Thread the wire through the slit and twist it until secure.

11. Using industrial-strength adhesive, adhere the flower to the same area of the toe. *Note: This will cover the wire.* Let glue dry. Apply superglue underneath the flower to further adhere to the toe.

12. Using superglue, adhere the small jewel stars to the heel.

13. Repeat Steps 7–12 with remaining shoe.

Laissez les bons temps roulez!

Metallic Ribbon Sandals

Expanding metallic ribbon has a wonderful ability to stretch out. Take advantage of this to create dimension in the loops on this sandal.

Accessories

Expanding metallic ribbon (5 yards)
Fabric scissors
Needle and invisible thread
Pair of strappy sandals

1. Cut the ribbon in half, reserving half for each shoe. Tie knots at the ends of each length of ribbon.

2. Stitch the knots onto the toe strap of one shoe. Distribute the ribbon evenly in loops across the toe. Stitch down the bottom of each loop to the strap so that it is secure.

3. Add dimension by pulling both sides of the loops to expand the ribbon. Expand the ends of the ribbon that extend out from the loops.

4. Repeat Steps 2–3 with remaining shoe.

Glitzy Sequined Heels

These shoes are decorated with pieces cut from a decorative wired embellishment. As it may be difficult to find something similar, keep your eye out for interesting embellishments at the craft store, fabric store, or even the thrift shop.

Accessories

Heavy decorative wired pieces or any desired
   embellishments (2)
Hot-glue gun and glue sticks
Pair of sequined sling-backs
Pins
Wire cutters

1. Cut pieces from the embellishment as desired and arrange them on the toe in a pleasing manner.

2. Glue the pieces onto the toe of the shoe in determined arrangement. Hold in place with pins until dry.

3. Repeat Steps 1–2 with remaining shoe.

Ribbon Canopy Sandals

These shoes have a "canopy" of ribbon that covers the strap.

Accessories

1½" x 2½" strips of black ribbon (2)
2½"–3"-wide striped ribbon
Adhesive dots
Craft knife
Fabric adhesive
Fabric scissors
Pair of high-heeled sandals
Straight pins
Tape measure

1. Measure the distance across the foot strap and add 1". Cut a length of the striped ribbon for each shoe to the determined measurement.

2. Place three evenly spaced adhesive dots on the foot strap. Adhere the striped ribbon across the foot strap, creating slight ripples with the ribbon at the adhesive dots for dimension.

3. Gather the ends of the ribbon a bit to make them narrower, then glue the ends to the bottom of the shoe with fabric adhesive. Hold in place with pins until the glue has dried.

4. Fold over the raw edges of the black ribbon and glue down to create neat edges. Glue the black ribbon across the bottom of the shoe, covering the ends of the striped ribbon.

5. Repeat Steps 2–4 with remaining shoe.

6. Measure the width and length of the toe strap. Cut a strip of the striped ribbon for each shoe to the determined measurement, adding approximately ⅛" to the width and the length.

7. Apply glue to the strip and adhere to the toe strap, making sure ribbon is centered. Fold under side edges. Use the craft knife to press the ends down where the strap meets the foot bed. Repeat with remaining shoe.

"I still have my feet on the ground, I just wear better shoes."
—Oprah Winfrey

something old, something new, something borrowed . . . and great shoes!

Walking Down the Aisle: Shoes for Brides and Bridesmaids

Whether you're a bride or a bridesmaid, finding the right pair of shoes for the wedding may be difficult. So take some time and decorate your own! Embellishing will take a pair of shoes from everyday plain to wedding-day beautiful.

Sophisticated Heels

Tiny glass marbles, available at crafts stores, add texture and a unique look to these dramatic Sophisticated Heels.

Accessories

¾" paintbrush
Alcohol
Cotton balls
Craft knife
Embossed fabric
Jewelry pieces such as brooches,
　earrings, or shoe clips (2)
Large bowl or pan
Pair of patent leather heels
Pencil
Plastic paint sealer
Rhinestones
Ribbon
Silk flowers
Superglue
Tiny glass marbles

1. Use a cotton ball to clean shoes with alcohol. Allow 30 minutes to one hour before applying paint.

2. Using pencil, trace Sophisticated Heels pattern on page 136 onto both sides of shoes.

3. Lay one shoe on scrap paper. Carefully squeeze superglue onto entire scroll pattern. Holding shoe over a large bowl or pan, pour marbles over shoe until all of glue is covered. Let glue dry. Repeat with remaining shoe.

4. Squeeze superglue onto the entire heel of the shoe. Cover with marbles as in Step 3. Repeat with remaining shoe.

5. Near the top of the heel, cut approximately ½" slit lengthwise on either side of the seam with craft knife. Thread sheer ribbon through both slits to the inside of the shoe and pull through until ribbon length is even on both sides. *Note: This ribbon will be used to tie up the ankle.*

Weave both sides of the ribbon through jewelry piece so that it sits just on top of the heel of the shoe. Tie ribbon in a knot to secure the jewelry piece.

6. Clip remaining jewelry piece onto toe at the instep.

7. Cut out a design from the embossed fabric. Glue onto the back of the heel as desired.

8. Glue the silk flowers onto the heel as desired.

9. Glue on rhinestones in desired pattern. Let glue dry.

10. Repeat Steps 5–9 with remaining shoe.

11. Apply two coats of plastic paint sealer to both shoes with ¾" paintbrush, allowing 45 minutes of drying time between coats.

"I don't know who invented the high heel, but all women owe him a lot."
—Marilyn Monroe

55

Lacy Floral Shoes and Stockings

To make the fancy stockings, sew fabric flowers in clusters to strips of lace, then glue the lace to the stockings with fabric glue. Place cans inside the stockings while gluing to prevent the stockings from sticking together. Use pearlescent fabric paint to add pearly dots.

Accessories

¼"-wide ecru silk satin ribbon (1 yard)

½"-wide vintage lace trim (½ yard)

¾"–1"-wide sequined or beaded floral motifs (8)

1"-wide peach silk satin ribbon (⅓ yard)

Double-sided adhesive sheets

Fabric scissors

Floral-motif vintage lace trim (⅜ yard)

Gem adhesive

Needle and ivory thread

Pair of fabric shoes

Pinking shears

Velvet leaves, pale blue (6) and light
   green/orchid (4)

Vintage flower spray (2)

Vintage lace pointed collar

1. Drape upper portion of one shoe with pointed collar tip. Trim to size and stitch in place.

2. Drape one side of shoe with the two satin ribbons to determine placement. Adhere with narrow strips cut from adhesive sheets.

3. Finish the edge of the lace collar with ½"-wide vintage lace trim, using double-sided adhesive to adhere the lace in place.

4. Tie a small bow with ¼"-wide satin ribbon. Glue or tape center of bow to beribboned side of shoe, then drape ribbon ends.

5. Using pinking shears, cut 18 small leaves from the light green/orchid leaves.

6. Arrange leaves as desired. Stitch or glue into place.

7. Cut floral lace motifs from floral-motif vintage trim. Using gem adhesive or needle and thread, secure lace motifs, flower spray, and sequined motifs onto the shoe.

8. Repeat Steps 1–7 with remaining shoe.

Button Pumps

Accessories

Craft scissors   Needle and ivory thread
Decorative buttons (2)   Pair of ivory pumps
Decorative wired trim   Superglue

1. Lay out trim on the shoe to determine placement. Cut a length for each shoe to determined measurement, plus a bit extra.

2. Thread the needle. Starting on the inside of one shoe, push the needle through the toe area, wrap it around the end of the decorative wire, and push it back through to secure the wire. While still inside, move the needle approximately 1" away and secure the wire again. Repeat this process until you have stitched the wire securely up the side of the shoe. Repeat with remaining shoe.

3. Place a drop of superglue on the inside and outside stitches of both shoes.

4. Glue the buttons to the desired area of the shoes.

Clay Roses Shoes

This is a very simple way to add style and elegance to a plain shoe.

Accessories

Clay roses and leaves
Decorative wired pearls
Industrial-strength adhesive
Pair of ivory mules
Pearl craft paint
Superglue

1. Determine desired location of clay roses on the toe of the shoe. Using industrial-strength adhesive, adhere the clay roses to desired location on both shoes. Let adhesive dry.

2. Place several drops of superglue underneath the roses to further secure. Glue wired pearls and clay leaves in desired locations.

White Roses Mules

Feminine and elegant, white roses are the perfect adornment for a bride's shoes.

Accessories

Craft scissors
Industrial-strength adhesive
Needle-nosed pliers
Net and pearl sprays (8)
Pair of white mules
Pearl and crystal sprays (6)
Small satin roses (72 blossoms)
Strong needle
Strong white thread
Thimble
Wire cutters

1. Arrange three pearl and crystal sprays and four net and pearl sprays as desired along the inner edge of the toe. Stitch the sprays onto the shoe.

2. Trim the wire ends, then bend the remainder away from the foot to avoid irritating the foot.

3. Using wire cutters, cut the rose blossoms from their wires. Glue them onto the shoe, covering the stitched area of the sprays. Follow the inner edge of the toe for placement. If desired, add height by piling the roses on top of each other and gluing in place.

4. Repeat Steps 1–3 with remaining shoe.

Floral Trim
Wedding Shoes

An embroidered floral motif and faux pearls create a wedding-day elegance on these shoes.

Accessories

Embroidered floral-motif fabric or trim

Fabric scissors

Industrial-strength adhesive

Pair of ivory sling-backs

Pearl beaded trim

Pearl beads

Superglue

1. Lay floral-motif fabric over the toe of one shoe to determine size needed. Cut a floral motif for each shoe to determined size from fabric.

2. Using superglue, glue the floral motif onto each shoe. Let glue dry.

3. Using industrial-strength adhesive, adhere pearl beads to areas of the floral motif as desired. *Note: This adhesive is thick, so it won't run and will allow enough time to put the pearls in place.*

4. Apply a line of industrial-strength adhesive along the perimeter of the top of one shoe. Adhere beaded trim. Let adhesive dry, then apply superglue along beaded trim to further secure. Repeat with remaining shoe.

"shoes are a girl's best friend."

—anonymous

Ribbon Flats and Hat

These flats look especially pretty with a hat made to match.

Accessories

Coordinating ribbon (2 yards)
Fabric scissors
Industrial-strength adhesive
Needle and matching thread
Pair of flats

1. Cut ribbon into two equal lengths. Straight-stitch along the edge of one length of ribbon. Pull thread to gather ribbon. As ribbon gathers, turn the gathers into a flower shape until flower becomes the desired size. Stitch around bottom of flower to secure. Knot the thread and trim the end. Leave excess ribbon attached. Repeat with remaining length of ribbon.

2. Stitch flower to the toe. Ripple the excess ribbon as you glue it around the shoe's top edge. Trim any excess ribbon where it meets with the flower. Repeat with remaining shoe.

Beaded Floral Sandals

Pastel shoes, such as these lavender heels, are perfect for adorning in beads and floral sprays.

Accessories

Craft scissors
Hot-glue gun and glue sticks
Pair of strappy sandals
Small beaded flowers
Sprays of small silk flowers
Strong needle and invisible thread

1. Cut small sprigs of flowers from sprays. Stitch approximately five sprigs across the toe straps, positioning the stems horizontally.

2. Hot-glue beaded flowers onto the sprays between the silk flowers.

Running Around:
Everyday Shoes

Whether you're at the office, at home, or running errands around town, these casual and dress shoes will add a little flair to your ordinary routine.

Ribbon Toe Mules

Before you start to apply the ribbons to the shoe, determine the direction the ribbon will go. Consider both shoes when you do this—try to avoid clashing directions.

Accessories

Craft knife
Craft scissors
Double-sided adhesive sheets
Pair of mules
Ribbon, enough to cover the toe of each shoe (3–4 yards)
Superglue
Water repellent (optional)

1. Place adhesive sheet over the toe of one shoe. Trace the area of the toe onto the adhesive sheet twice. Cut out pieces.

2. Remove paper backing from one side of the adhesive pieces. Apply ribbon strips to the pieces, laying them side by side and making sure the edges are flush.

3. Remove the remaining backing and adhere the ribbon sheets tightly and smoothly to the toes of the shoes. Allow excess ribbon to go beyond the length of the toe. Crease the ribbon at the edges of the soles. Using the craft knife, cut along the crease lines to remove the excess ribbon. Apply a line of superglue along the edges of the soles. Press the ribbon ends into the glue to secure.

4. At the instep of the shoes where there is overlapping ribbon, trim the ribbon that extends past the insteps to approximately ½". Fold the ends under to the insides of the shoes.

5. Cut two pieces from ribbon for each shoe to fit inside the toe. Cut ends on an angle so that ends line up with angle of foot bed. Using strips of adhesive sheets, adhere the ribbon into the shoes, covering the ends that were folded over.

6. If desired, spray the shoes with water repellent to prevent staining.

Polka Dot Shoes and Purse

These are such easy shoes to make. Because the paint adheres to the fabric so well, there is no prep work or finish work.

Accessories

Acrylic paint	Pair of fabric shoes
Fabric purse	Pencil
New pencil with eraser	Ruler

1. Using the ruler and pencil, measure and mark the desired location of the polka dots on the shoes. *Note: This helps to create a more planned design for a finished look.*

2. Dip end of eraser into paint and dot onto fabric at determined locations. Let paint dry.

3. Follow Steps 1–2 to place polka dots on the purse.

Floral Butterfly Shoes

Create a garden at your feet with painted flowers and butterflies.

Accessories

³⁄₄" paintbrush	Paintbrushes
Acrylic paints	Pair of leather mules
Alcohol	Pencil
Brown fine-line permanent marker	Plastic paint primer
	Plastic paint sealer
Cotton balls	

1. Clean shoes with cotton ball and alcohol.

2. Paint shoes with two coats of primer, using ³⁄₄" brush, allowing 15 minutes drying time between coats. Rinse brush. Allow 30 minutes to one hour before applying paint.

3. Draw desired design onto shoes in pencil. Paint in images. *Note: It may take a few coats to get the coverage desired.* Let paint dry.

4. Use marker to outline details.

5. Paint shoes with two coats of sealer, using ³⁄₄" brush, allowing 45 minutes drying time between coats.

Suede Flats

You can decorate these shoes in whatever shapes you desire. Use stencils or simply cut them out freehand.

Accessories

Craft scissors
Hot-glue gun and glue sticks
Pair of suede flats
Permanent marker
Scrap leather
Sequins

1. Cut out shapes, such as stars and hearts, from scrap leather. Decorate the shapes as desired with permanent marker.

2. Hot-glue leather shapes as desired onto shoes.

3. Hot-glue sequins as desired onto leather shapes.

Pretty Pink Moccasins

Accessories

Awl

Craft scissors

Large "crystal" buttons (2)

Large-eyed needle

Leather glue

Narrow gold-edged ribbon (1½ yards)

Pair of pink moccasins with original cord removed

1. Thread needle with ribbon. Stitch ribbon through cord holes along one side of the shoe, then glue ribbon to the side. Trim ends as necessary. Apply glue to the ends, then use awl to insert ends into end holes. Repeat on remaining side of shoe.

2. Thread needle with a length of ribbon. Knot the end. Stitch ribbon through holes along the shoe toe and secure end with a knot.

3. Thread a length of ribbon through button. Loop each side of the ribbon through the corresponding side hole several times. Knot the ends.

4. Create six loops from ribbon and glue the ends of three loops under each side of the button. Let dry.

5. Repeat Steps 1–4 with remaining shoe.

71

Wooden Bead Moccasins

Natural motifs, like wooden leaf cutouts, are the perfect accompaniment for down-to-earth moccasins.

Accessories

Awl (optional)
Cord
Hot-glue gun and glue sticks
Pair of moccasins
Small wooden star beads
Wooden bell beads
Wooden leaf cutouts

1. Hot-glue wooden leaf cutouts onto toes.

2. Starting from underneath, thread cord through holes in top of one moccasin. *Note: If the moccasin does not have holes, use awl to make two.* Thread ends through bell beads, then tie ends into knots. Trim any excess. Tie cord into a square knot. Repeat with remaining shoe.

3. Hot-glue star beads along the sides of shoes.

"May your moccasins make happy tracks in many snows, and may the rainbow always touch your shoulder."
—Cherokee prayer

Coil Braid Flats

For these shoes, use a narrow trim that is easy to coil.

Accessories

Fabric scissors
Glass beads (2)
Hot-glue gun and glue
   sticks

Narrow braided trim
Pair of flats

1. Lay trim along shoe instep twice and coil into a circle at the toe to determine length needed. Add 2", then cut a length from trim for each shoe to the determined length.

2. Glue trim along perimeter of shoe instep twice, beginning at center front and working around to center again.

3. Coil the remaining trim at the toe, starting with the inside of the coil and working out. Glue the underside of the trim to the toe as you go. Trim excess.

4. Hot-glue glass bead to coil center.

5. Repeat Steps 2–4 with remaining shoe.

Have Passport, Will Travel Sneakers

Adhering photos, ephemera, and old passport pages to a pair of shoes is a fun way to preserve memories from a favorite trip. Just make sure any passport pages you use have neither identifying numbers nor unexpired visas.

Accessories

Computer, paper, printer, and scanner (optional)

Craft scissors

Decorative trim (4 yards)

Fabric adhesive

Fabric markers (optional)

Fine-grit sandpaper (optional)

Maps, tickets, photos, and old passport pages
    from a favorite trip

Pair of canvas high-top sneakers

Small paintbrush

Tape (optional)

1. Scan and print color copies of photos, maps, and old passport pages, or copy them at a copy center.

2. Determine desired arrangement of the pages and images by first arranging them on a table, then on the sneakers themselves. Set the images side by side or overlap them as desired. *Note: You can temporarily tape some images into place to help determine arrangement.* Trim the photos to the desired size and shape.

3. Working one area at a time, use the paintbrush to cover shoes with fabric adhesive. Press images firmly on top of the area, making sure every bit is glued securely. Continue the process until the shoes are covered as desired. *Note: You may want to leave the shoelace area alone because the holes can be difficult to work with.*

4. Coat all the images with the fabric adhesive. Let adhesive dry.

5. If desired, gently sand the dried adhesive with sandpaper for a leathery look.

6. Use fabric markers to add a dash of color if desired, or to change the color of any exposed canvas.

7. For a more finished look, glue trim along any ragged or plain edges.

Dangling Beads Moccasins

The beads used here were taken from an old Christmas tree garland. You can use beads from old pieces of jewelry as well, or you can purchase them at a bead store.

Accessories

20-gauge gold wire
Beading thread or invisible thread
Decorative beads
Headpins (6)
Long-nosed pliers
Pair of moccasins or suede shoes
Strong beading needle

1. String beads onto headpins. Using pliers, bend the open ends into a loop.

2. Using pliers, create two decorative "S" shapes with gold wire. Stitch both sides of each piece onto outsides of the shoes at the seam.

3. Hook looped ends of headpins onto the "S" shapes, using three per shoe.

Leopard Toe Flats

Satin rope trim adds an urban flair to a pair of animal-print shoes.

Accessories

Beads

Fabric scissors

Industrial-strength
  adhesive

Pair of flats with
  animal print design

Satin rope trim

1. Place trim around the toe of one shoe to determine amount needed. Repeat for the length around the instep, adding 4". Cut lengths from trim for each shoe to determined measurements.

2. Glue the short length of trim around the toe of the shoe at the seam line.

3. Starting 2" from the end, glue the long trim around the instep. *Note: When you reach the other side, you should have 2" left over.*

4. Coil the extra 2" on each side and glue down where the top of the toe and the side meet. Tuck the end under the coil and secure with glue.

5. Glue the beads on the coils as desired.

6. Repeat Steps 2–5 with remaining shoe.

Jacquard Heels

This pair of slides is adorned in sumptuous fabric.

Accessories

⅛"-wide grosgrain or other ribbon trim (approximately 1½ yards)	Lettuce-edged trim (approximately 1 yard)
Craft scissors	Paper and pencil
Double-sided adhesive sheets	Scrap of muslin
	Scroll gimp trim (approximately 1 yard)
Fabric scissors	
Gem adhesive	Shoe suitable to be
Jacquard fabric	covered with fabric

1. Drape upper portion of shoe with muslin to create a pattern. Trace shoe lines onto draped muslin with a pencil.

2. Cut out muslin on traced lines. Replace muslin onto shoe to check pattern. Adjust as necessary.

3. Make a paper pattern from the muslin pattern. Cut out jacquard fabric according to pattern.

4. Cut a 1"-wide strip of adhesive sheet to fit front of shoe, from toe to instep. Center the strip and adhere onto front of shoe. Cut ½"-wide strips from tape and position on upper shoe at sole line and instep.

5. Remove paper backing from adhesive sheet. Position fabric in place on shoe, pulling fabric taut and smooth. Trim any excess fabric.

6. Cover heel with fabric in the same manner, if desired. Finish raw edges with trims, using adhesive sheets to adhere.

7. Using gem adhesive, glue ⅛"-wide ribbon around lower edge of upper shoe at sole line to create a clean finish.

8. Cut a ¼"-wide strip of adhesive sheet. Position along instep edge. Remove adhesive sheet covering and position lettuce-edged trim onto tape, creating a clean finish at the instep. Make certain to tape under raw edges of trim in the process.

9. Tape or glue gimp trim over edge of lettuce trim.

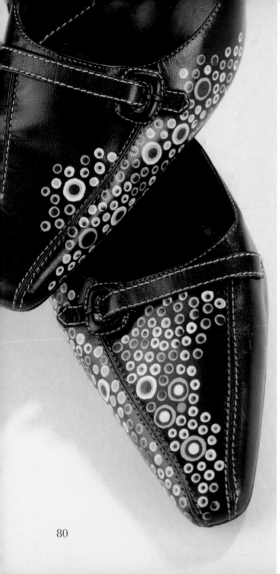

Dotted Shoes

The circles on these shoes are easy to make with the ends of paintbrushes and pencil erasers.

Accessories

³/₄" paintbrushes

Acetone

Acrylic paints in dark brown, ivory, and sandstone

Cotton balls

Liner/script paintbrush

New pencil with eraser

Pair of leather flats

Plastic paint primer

Plastic paint sealer

1. Rub area of shoes you will be painting with a cotton ball dipped in acetone.

2. Paint two thin coats of plastic paint primer on the shoes with ³/₄" paintbrush, allowing 15 minutes of drying time between coats. Rinse brush. Allow 30 minutes to one hour before applying paint.

3. Make large dots on the shoes by dipping the pencil eraser in ivory paint and dotting in desired pattern on shoes. Wipe off paint from eraser. Make additional large dots with eraser dipped in sandstone. Let paint dry.

4. Using the handle end of ³/₄" paintbrush, make ivory dots as desired, placing some inside the large sandstone dots. Make additional dots with sandstone as desired, placing some in the center of the large ivory dots.

5. Using the handle end of the liner/script paintbrush, make dark brown dots as desired, placing some in the centers of the sandstone dots. Let paint dry completely.

6. Paint shoes with two coats of plastic paint sealer, using ³/₄" paintbrush, allowing 45 minutes of drying time between coats.

"Keep your eyes on the stars,
and your feet on the ground."
—Theodore Roosevelt

Stars and Stripes Pumps

We used red ribbon with white stitching for these pumps. The red adds punch to the sophistication of the black, white, and silver.

Accessories

½"-wide ribbon with stitching along sides (30")
½"-wide silver textured star buttons (16)
Craft knife
Fabric scissors
Industrial-strength adhesive
Pair of patterned fabric pumps
Pencil
Wire cutters

1. Mark the desired location of the ribbon on each shoe. *Note: Make sure that the ribbons run parallel to each other and that the shoes are identical to each other regarding placement.* Measure the amount of ribbon needed and add 1". Cut lengths from ribbon for each shoe to determined measurement.

2. Apply glue to the ribbon, stopping ½" from each end. Place ribbon on the shoes in the determined location, making sure that ½" extends past the edge of the soles on each side.

3. Crease the ribbon at the edge of the soles. Using the craft knife, cut along the crease line to remove the excess ribbon. Apply a line of superglue along the edge of the soles. Press the ribbon ends into the glue to secure.

4. Using wire cutters, cut the button shank from the back of each star button. *Note: Cut as close to the back of the button as possible.* Lay several buttons onto the shoe between the red ribbons to determine the spacing. Mark placement if desired.

5. Apply sufficient glue to each star to secure it to the shoe, making sure that the glue doesn't seep out around the star. *Note: You can align the stars so that they all point the same way, or you can point them at random.* Let glue dry.

6. Glue a single star to the outside of each heel. Let glue dry.

These boots were made for walking!

Walking Tall: Boots

It's hard not to notice a great pair of
boots — especially when those boots
are as fun, funky, and
dramatic as these.
Slip on a pair and go
get yourself noticed!

Heirloom Boots

Use old family photos for these boots. Every time you wear them, you'll have your family at your feet!

Accessories

Computer, paper, printer, and scanner (optional)
Craft scissors
Decorative trim (5 yards)
Fabric (1/2 yard)
Fabric protector
Fabric scissors
Imitation gold chain (30") (optional)
Metallic-colored acrylic paint (optional)
Old family photos
Pair of heeled boots
Permanent fabric adhesive
Thin flexible trim (12")
Wire cutters (optional)

1. Examine the boots, taking note of the various pattern pieces that were used to put them together. Cut fabric into shapes that will cover and match each pattern piece of each boot. *Note: You may want to leave the shoelace area alone because the holes can be difficult to work with.*

2. If using the gold chain, cut two 5" lengths and two 10" lengths, using the scissors or wire cutters.

3. Drape a 5" chain at the back of the boot over the heel. Spacing the ends approximately 2" apart, glue 1" of each end onto the shoe so that the chain drapes down across the heel. Repeat with remaining boot.

4. Using fabric adhesive, adhere fabric over the different sections of boots. *Note: If using the gold chain, apply the fabric on top of the chain so that the chain will be anchored in place.*

5. If using the gold chain, glue one end of a 10" length to the top edge of the boot at the front, where the fabric meets the shoelace area. Glue the middle of the chain to the back of the top edge. Glue the remaining end where the fabric meets the shoelace area on the other side of the boot. Repeat with remaining boot.

6. Glue the trim along the top edges of the boots, making sure to cover the three areas where the chain is adhered. Adhere trim along the ragged edges of each panel piece.

7. Scan and print old family photos or copy them at a copy center. *Note: You can also create an iron-on transfer. See the Designer Tip on page 18.*

8. Cut the photos into desired shapes. Using fabric adhesive, glue them onto the inside and outside panels of boots.

9. Glue the thin, flexible trim around the photos as a frame.

10. If desired, enhance the shoelaces with acrylic paint. Dip your thumb and forefinger into paint, then quickly run the shoelaces between your fingers so that the paint creates smudges of color. Let paint dry.

11. To protect boots, spray them with fabric protector.

Spotted Boots and Hat

These funky boots and hat are simply enhanced by fuzzy eyelash trim.

Accessories

Fuzzy eyelash trim
Matching hat
Matching trim for hat
Needle and matching thread
Pair of spotted animal print boots

1. Slip-stitch fuzzy eyelash trim around the top of the boot. If the boot has a zipper, start and end the trim at the zipper.

2. Secure each end of the trim by stitching around the end to prevent fraying.

3.Tie the fuzzy eyelash trim around the base of the hat crown. Tie the matching trim around the fuzzy trim at the side of the hat. Secure with needle and thread if necessary.

Beaded Animal Stripe Boots

It's a jungle out there, so make sure you're equipped with the right attire. These animal stripe boots are jazzed up with beaded fringe.

Accessories

Craft scissors
Industrial-strength adhesive
Needle and matching thread
Pair of striped animal print boots
Ribbon with beaded fringe

1. Place the ribbon around the top of the boot to determine amount needed. Cut a length from ribbon for each boot to determined measurement.

2. Stitch ribbon along inside of one boot at the top so that beads dangle over the top. Glue down the ends to prevent fraying or loss of beads. Repeat with remaining boot.

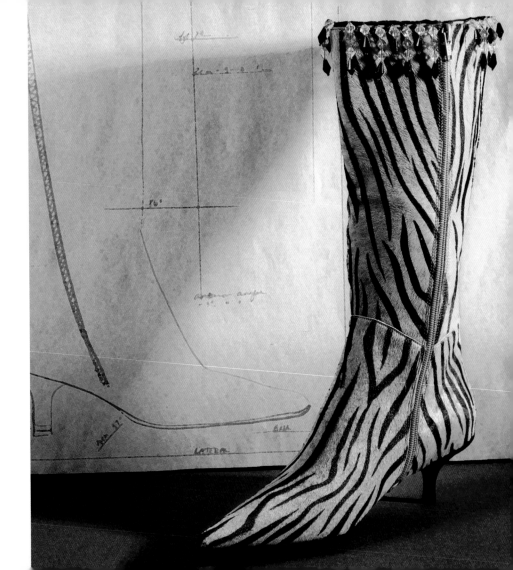

Bead Dangle Boots and Hat

Look for a pair of boots with knit cuffs for this project—it is so easy to sew the beaded trim onto the fabric, plus you can fold over the cuffs to hide the stitching.

Accessories

Beaded trim

Fabric scissors

Matching hat

Needle and matching thread

Pair of boots with knit cuffs

1. Stitch the beaded ribbon to the inside of the unfolded cuff. Stitch somewhat loosely to accommodate the stretch of the knit cuff. Fold over the cuff. Repeat with remaining boot.

2. Cut a length of beaded trim, long enough to form a bundle of beads. Roll top of trim into a tight roll and stitch together. Stitch to the brim of the hat so that the beads dangle off the hat.

Rhinestone Buckle Boots

The same sheer ribbon of these sophisticated boots can be used to adorn a matching hat.

Accessories

2"-wide sheer ribbon
Double-sided
    adhesive sheets
Fabric scissors

Pair of black boots
Silver rhinestone
    buckles (2)
Tape measure

1. Measure circumference of boot at the ankle. Add 3". Cut a length from ribbon for each boot to determined measurement.

2. Thread ribbon through buckle so that 1" of ribbon extends past the buckle bar. Fold the end over the bar and attach to back side of ribbon with adhesive sheet.

3. Wrap the ribbon around the boot ankle, positioning the buckle on the outside. Thread remaining end of ribbon through the buckle and extend it out the other side. Attach the ribbon underneath where it crosses over the buckle bar. Trim the end to the desired length.

4. Repeat Steps 2–3 with remaining boot.

"Cute as a Button" Boots

Splashing through puddles is even more fun in a cute pair of boots like these.

Accessories

Beading thread or invisible thread

Black-and-white striped cotton fabric

Buttons in various colors and sizes

Fabric scissors

Industrial-strength adhesive

Iron

Pair of children's rubber boots

Rickrack in assorted colors

Strong needle

Tape measure

1. Measure the inside circumference of the boot, adding about 1". Cut a piece from the black-and-white striped fabric for each boot to the determined length, with a width of 5".

2. Using iron, press the long sides and one short side of one piece of fabric over 1" to create a neat edge. Glue wrong side of fabric to the inside of one boot, extending the fabric ½" past the top edge of the boot. Where the two ends of the fabric meet, overlap the ends and glue down. To accommodate the taper at the leg of the boot, cut several slits into the lining, overlapping at these points as needed to ensure a good fit. Let glue dry. Repeat with remaining boot.

3. Wrap three colors of rickrack around the center of the boots. *Note: You can measure so that each colored stripe is at the same level on each shoe, or you can deliberately attach the rickrack at different levels.* Glue rickrack onto boots. Let glue dry.

4. Stitch the rickrack onto the black-and-white fabric around the tops of the boots.

5. Stitch buttons to the rickrack around the tops of the boots, overlapping them and varying the height of each.

6. Glue buttons as desired to the center pieces of rickrack.

The pitter patter
of little feet . . .

Baby Steps:
Shoes for Little Ones

There aren't many things in the world
cuter than baby shoes—except for
babies themselves, of course. Whether
you spend time sewing shoes,
or just add paint to a
purchased pair,
the results will
be adorable.

Bright Toddler Slippers

Have fun picking out interesting patterns and colors of fabric for these cute slippers.

Accessories

¼"-thick x 8"-square foam
⅜"-wide elastic (12")
1"-wide pleated grosgrain ribbon (12")
6" x 15" sherpa fabric
8" x 16" bright striped fabric
8" x 16" fusible fleece
8" x 16" print fabric
8"-square velveteen fabric
8"-square faux zebra fur fabric
Fabric scissors
Iron and ironing board
Needle and matching threads
Pink and green rosettes (2)
Sewing machine and matching threads
Straight pins
Tailor's chalk

1. Using the Bright Toddler Slippers patterns on page 135, trace sole pattern twice each onto velveteen fabric and faux zebra fur. Cut out.

2. Trace the sole pattern twice onto the foam. Cut out, trimming off the ¼" seam allowance.

3. Trace toe pattern twice each onto striped fabric and print fabric. Cut out.

4. Trace toe pattern twice onto fusible fleece. Cut out, trimming off the ¼" seam allowance from all edges.

5. Trace heel pattern twice onto sherpa fabric. Cut out.

6. Using iron, adhere fleece to wrong side of striped toe pieces. Place striped toe pieces and print fabric pieces together, with right sides facing. Sew along the inner curved edge, using a ¼" seam allowance. Clip curves to seam line. Using iron, press the seam allowance open. Turn right side out. Press with iron. Topstitch close to seam line.

7. Baste-stitch outer curved edges together, using a machine-gathering-stitch.

8. Cut elastic into two 6" lengths. Pin elastic to wrong side of heel pieces, placing the elastic just below the fold line indicated on the pattern. Machine-zigzag in place through the center of the elastic.

9. With right sides facing, pin toe to heel at side edges, aligning side edge of toe with lower curved side of heel. *Note: Heel fold line indicated on pattern should line up with top edge of toe piece.* Fold heel piece over on fold line and pin onto lining side of toe. Sew side edges together, using ¼" seam allowance. Turn right side out. Press with iron.

10. Machine-baste-stitch outer edges of heel together.

11. Pull gathering threads on toe sections. Pin lining side of heel/toe to right side of inner sole, adjusting toe gathers to fit sole between square dots. Sew heel/toe to sole, using ¼" seam allowance, leaving the opening at center back where indicated by dots on pattern.

12. Turn inner sole/heel/toe inside out. Pin outer sole to inner sole, right sides facing. Sew together using ¼" seam allowance, leaving the opening at center back where indicated by dots on pattern.

13. Sew again ¹⁄₁₆" from first row of stitching. Trim seam allowance close to second row of stitching. Turn right side out through back opening.

14. Slip foam into space between inner and outer soles.

15. Pin back end of outer sole and heel together, right sides facing, taking a ¼" seam allowance. Sew again ⅛" from first row of stitching. Trim seam allowance and machine-overcast.

16. Hand-stitch pleated ribbon trim to inner edge of toe. Hand-stitch rosette centered over ribbon trim.

Vintage Print Baby Shoes

Accessories

½" buttons (2)
1⅜" x 9¼" contrasting print cotton fabric cut on bias (2)
5"-square chenille fabric
9" x 12" vintage print fabric
4mm silk ribbon (¾ yard)
Cotton print fabric (¼ yard)
Cream thread
Fabric scissors
Iron and ironing board
Satin cord (1 yard)
Sewing machine
Size 3 embroidery needle
Tape measure

1. Using Print Baby Shoes patterns on page 136, trace sole pattern onto chenille and vintage fabrics, one facing left and one facing right on each fabric. Cut out.

2. Trace upper shoe pattern twice each onto vintage print fabric and cotton print fabric. Cut out.

3. Cut four 1⅜" x 12½" bias strips from cotton print fabric. Seam together two bias strips for each shoe along short edges. Fold strips in half lengthwise, wrong sides together, then press with iron. *Note: When working with the pressed bias strip, the raw edges are treated as one edge.*

4. Place wrong sides of one chenille and one vintage print sole pieces together. With chenille fabric side up, match raw edges of bias strip with outer edges of sole and sew together, using a ⅛" seam allowance. Begin and end sewing at sole center back. Sew the bias seam line at sole center back, trimming off excess to ¼" seam allowance. Press seam allowance toward bias strip. Fold bias strip over seam allowance and onto print side of sole. Sew bias strip in place, enclosing seam allowance. Repeat with the remaining chenille and vintage print sole pieces.

5. Fold a vintage print upper shoe piece in half, right sides facing. Sew the back seam, using ¼" seam allowance. Repeat with remaining vintage print upper shoe piece and the two cotton print upper shoe pieces.

6. Place one vintage print and one cotton print upper shoe pieces together, with wrong sides facing. With vintage print side up, bind lower edges together with bias strip as in Step 4. Repeat with remaining vintage print and cotton print upper shoe pieces.

7. Working with the contrasting cotton print bias strips, fold one bias in half, matching short ends. Seam short ends, using ¼" seam allowance. Press seam allowance open. Press piece in half lengthwise. Repeat with remaining bias strip.

8. Gather-stitch upper shoes between dots indicated on pattern. Pull gather stitches so that gathered space measures 2¾".

9. With vintage print side up, bind upper edges together with contrasting cotton print bias strip as in Step 4. Repeat with remaining upper shoe pieces.

10. With insides facing, whipstitch outer bias edge of sole to outer bias edge of upper shoe. Repeat with remaining sole and upper shoe pieces.

11. Cut 4mm ribbon into two lengths. Thread one length into embroidery needle. Beginning at front center of upper shoe, hand-stitch around upper shoe just below bias binding seam line. Pull stitches in order to gather upper edge of upper shoe a bit so that opening measures approximately 7½" all the way around. Tie ribbon ends into knot. Slip ribbon ends through button and tie ends into knot again to secure button in place.

12. Cut satin cord into two lengths. Fold one length in half to find center. Stitch center to upper shoe center back upper edge. Knot satin cord ends.

13. Repeat Steps 11–12 with the remaining shoe.

"Little Betty Blue
Lost her holiday shoe.
Give her another
To match the other
And then she'll walk upon two."
—Unknown

Puffy Paint Sneakers

Dimensional fabric paints are great for adding texture and color to kids' shoes.

Accessories

Pair of children's canvas shoes
Variety of dimensional fabric paints

1. Remove the shoelaces.

2. Determine the desired paint colors for the shoe. If desired, practice with the paints on a piece of paper.

3. Place the shoe on a piece of paper so that you can rotate it while painting. Paint lines and dots on the shoe, one color at a time, making sure to leave space between the lines and dots to allow other colors to be inserted. *Note: The lines will overlap. Try not to let the paint blur at each crossing point.* Continue in this manner until you achieve desired look. Let paint dry completely before lacing up shoes.

Green Sherpa Booties

These booties are as soft as they are adorable.

Accessories

3/8"-wide elastic (12")
Darning needle
Fabric scissors
Iron and ironing board
Mint green faux suede/sherpa fabric (1/8 yard)
Needle and matching thread
Pink butterfly beads
Sewing machine
Straight pins
Tailor's chalk

1. Using Green Sherpa Booties patterns on page 137, trace heel pattern, sole pattern, and toe pattern onto green faux suede/sherpa fabric, once for each shoe.

2. Cut slashes into toe pieces where indicated on pattern.

3. Machine-zigzag-stitch around edges of heel/sole pieces, then toe/sole pieces.

4. Fold down heel cuff, fold heel pieces on fold line indicated on pattern, placing sherpa side of fabric toward the outside. Sew cuff to heel, stitching 1/4" upward from heel straight edge, forming a casing for the elastic.

5. With sherpa sides facing, pin a heel section to a sole section, matching center back dots and aligning the heel seam line square dots with the square dots on the sole. Sew pieces together, using a 1/8" seam allowance. Repeat for the remaining heel and sole pieces.

6. Cut elastic into two 6" lengths. Slip elastic lengths in and out of slashes on toe section. Leave ends loose.

7. With sherpa sides facing, pin a toe piece to a sole piece, matching center front dots and aligning the toe seam lines x's with the x's on the sole. Sew pieces together, using a 1/8" seam allowance. *Note: The toe seam line will overlap the heel seam line for a space of about 7/8". Repeat for the remaining toe piece.*

8. Use darning needle to slip elastic through cuff casings. Sew elastic ends together and then maneuver elastic seam allowance so that it is hidden within the casings.

9. Stitch butterfly bead to toe center front, covering visible section of elastic.

Wool Baby Shoes

Accessories

¼"-wide light blue cotton ribbon (1 yard)
Cream thread
Darning needle
Embroidery floss in cream (optional) and light blue
Fabric scissors
Iron and ironing board
Sewing machine
Size 5 embroidery needle
Straight pins
Tailor's chalk
Washable wool in ecru (4" x 10") and navy (7" x 7")

1. Using Wool Baby Shoes patterns on page 136, trace toe onto ecru wool twice. Cut out.

2. Trace sole pattern onto navy wool twice, one facing left and one facing right. Trace heel pattern onto navy wool twice. Cut out.

3. Machine-sew a decorative buttonhole stitch around all edges of each shoe piece, using cream thread. *Note: You can also do the stitch by hand, using three strands of cream embroidery floss.* Using iron, press each embroidered section.

4. Using embroidery needle and three strands of light blue embroidery floss and a straight stitch, embroider a star on each toe section where indicated on toe pattern.

5. With wrong sides facing, pin a heel section to the left-facing sole section, matching center-back dots and aligning the heel seam line square dots with the square dots on the sole.

6. With wrong sides facing, pin a toe section to the left-facing sole section, matching center-front dots and aligning the toe seam line x's with the x's on the sole. *Note: The toe seam line will overlap the heel seam line by ½".*

7. Using cream thread and a decorative machine-double-straight-stitch, sew toe and heel to sole, with a ¹⁄₁₆" seam allowance. *Note: You can also do the stitch by hand.*

8. Repeat Steps 5–7 for the right-facing sole section.

9. Using darning needle, thread ribbon or shoelaces through upper edges of heel and toe where indicated by dotted lines on heel pattern and toe pattern. Tie knots at ribbon ends, then tie ribbon into bows. Repeat with remaining shoe.

Designer Tip:

Washable wool is a wonderful fabric for baby shoes because it is warm, durable, comes in soft colors, and, of course, is washable! The fabric is also easy to work with and holds its shape well. Look for it at your local fabric store.

Suede/Sherpa Booties

Soft and warm, faux suede/sherpa fabric makes a wonderful pair of winter booties.

Accessories

$5/16$" vintage flat ball buttons (2)
$3/8$"-wide elastic ($10\frac{1}{2}$")
$3/8$"-wide lettuce-edged embroidered trim (1 yard)
$3/8$"-wide vintage lace ($1\frac{1}{2}$ yards)
Fabric scissors
Faux suede/sherpa fabric ($1/4$ yard)
Iron and ironing board
Needle and matching thread
Sewing machine
Tape measure

1. Using Suede/Sherpa Booties patterns on page 137, trace sole pattern, tongue pattern, and upper shoe pattern onto faux suede/sherpa fabric, twice for each pattern. Cut out.

2. Machine-zigzag-stitch around all edges of each cut fabric piece.

3. Cut elastic into two $5\frac{1}{4}$" lengths. Machine-zigzag-stitch elastic to sherpa side of upper shoe pieces on line indicated on pattern, stretching the elastic to fit the length of the area while sewing.

4. Working from the faux suede side of fabric, sew the edge of the lace trim to the edges of tongue and upper shoe pieces where indicated on the patterns, using a narrow machine-zigzag stitch. Press lace, using proper iron setting so as to not imprint or melt faux suede and sherpa.

5. With sherpa sides facing, sew a tongue section to a sole, matching center-front dots, using a $1/8$" seam allowance. Align the tongue seam line square dots with the square dots on the sole. Repeat with remaining tongue and sole pieces.

6. With sherpa sides facing, sew an upper shoe piece to a sole piece, matching center-back dots, using a $1/8$" seam allowance. Align the upper shoe seam line x's with the x's on the sole, overlapping the upper shoe piece onto tongue. *Note: The upper shoe seam line will overlap the tongue seam line by approximately $7/8$". Repeat with remaining upper shoe piece.*

7. Cut lettuce-edged trim into four 9" lengths. Working with one piece, make a loop with 1" of trim, folding end under $1/4$". Sew loop to front edge of upper shoe at elastic line, making sure to sew down the $1/4$". Sew another length to the upper shoe on the opposite front edge in the same manner. Repeat for the remaining upper shoe piece. Tie ends into a small bow.

8. Stitch a loop with thread on upper shoe where indicated on pattern. Stitch button to upper shoe where indicated on pattern. Button upper shoe closed. Repeat with remaining bootie.

9. Fold upper part of each bootie down, forming a small cuff.

Fancy Footwork:
A Gallery of Shoes as Art

Once clumsy and utilitarian, shoes today have evolved into not only emblems of fashion, but also works of art. Our fascination with footwear has driven artists to explore the possibilities of these everyday items, turning them into objects of beauty, whimsy, and creativity.

Persimmon Froglette's Toe Shoes

Tuck an old paper doll and theater tickets into these embellished shoes and enjoy the show!

Accessories

¼"-wide pink silk ribbon (2 yards)

½" foam brushes

Craft scissors

Decorative scroll patterned paper

Decoupage medium

Faux pearls (2)

Gesso

Glitter

Hole punch

Hot-glue gun and glue sticks

Needle and matching thread

Old book print

Pair of vintage leather ballet slippers

Pink crepe paper

Spenserian script patterned paper

White glue

1. Remove the slipper insoles. Trace one right and one left insole onto Spenserian script paper for insoles. Repeat on decorative scrolls paper for soles. Cut out. Set aside decorative scroll soles.

2. Using foam brush and decoupage medium, decoupage Spenserian script insoles directly over shoe insoles. Let dry.

3. Using the foam brush, apply one coat of gesso to the interior and exterior of the shoes.

4. Tear old book print into ½" x 1" strips. Starting at back heel area on interior of one shoe, decoupage all the way around, laying each strip next to the last. Let dry. Repeat with remaining shoe.

5. Hot-glue insoles into the shoes.

6. Cut crepe paper into ½" x 1" strips and decoupage on the exterior of one shoe, starting at heel and going all the way around. Apply three layers of crepe paper, letting each layer dry well before starting the next. Let dry. Repeat with remaining shoe.

7. Hot-glue decorative scroll soles to the bottom of the slippers.

8. Make glitter dots by brushing a thin layer of white glue on a sheet of paper, then sprinkling it with glitter. When dry, punch out the glitter dots with a hole punch and glue onto the shoes as desired with white glue.

9. Make two florets out of crepe paper and glue onto centers of shoes. Embellish center of florets with a faux pearl. Add dots of glitter by applying small dots of glue, then sprinkling with glitter before glue dries. Tap shoe to remove excess glitter.

10. Cut pink silk ribbon into four equal lengths. Stitch a length along the top edge on either side of the heels.

Baby Mouse Booties

With decoupaged decorative paper and a little mouse paper doll, this is a sweet pair of baby booties to be cherished.

Accessories

½" foam brush
2" x 8" strip of crepe paper
Book print
Craft scissors
Decoupage medium
Gesso
Pair of baby booties
Pinking shears
Scrap of old lace
Small awl
Variety of coordinating decorative papers
Vintage paper doll
White glue

1. Remove shoelaces.

2. Using foam brush, apply a coat of gesso to the booties. Let gesso dry completely.

3. Trace the bottom of the bootie onto book print four times. Cut out.

4. Decoupage the book print cutouts onto the interior and exterior of each sole.

5. Tear pieces from decorative papers into ½" squares. Using foam brush and decoupage medium, decoupage the squares onto the interior and exterior of the booties, letting the papers extend ¼" past the top edge. Let dry, then trim top edge with pinking shears.

6. Punch out shoelace holes with awl. Lace up the booties.

7. Apply a line of white glue down the center of the crepe paper strip. Roll into a tight ball. Let dry completely. Repeat this three more times. Glue crepe paper balls onto the ends of shoelaces.

8. Embellish the paper doll with lace. Slip the paper doll into one shoe.

"You want to fall in love with a shoe, go ahead. A shoe can't love you back, but, on the other hand, a shoe can't hurt you too deeply either. And there are so many nice-looking shoes."

—Allan Sherman

In-love Doves Wedding Shoes

The adornments on these shoes are actually photo-copied right off the sleeve of a European gown, circa 1880s. Lace and book print copied together create a wonderful trompe l'oeil effect as well.

Accessories

½" foam brush
15-gauge wire
26-gauge wire
Book print
Cardstock
Craft scissors
Decoupage medium
Decorative-edged
  scissors
Excelsior
Feathers
Gesso
Glitter
Hot-glue gun and
  glue sticks

Pair of spool-heel
  leather shoes
Pencil
Photocopier
Piece of lace
Pliers
Printer paper
Rhinestones
Ribbon
Various decorative
  papers, including a
  garden/nature motif
Vintage pearls
White crepe paper
White glue
Wire cutters

1. Using pliers, bend the 15-gauge wire into a large heart shape. Bend ends into swirls to clip onto shoes.

2. Wind crepe paper around the heart and adhere with white glue.

3. To make fringe, stack several strips of crepe paper, fold in half lengthwise, and make tiny cuts all the way across, leaving ¼" uncut along the center edge.

4. Fluff up the fringe and glue onto the heart with white glue.

5. To make ivy leaves, cut several 6" pieces of 26-gauge wire. Cut heart-shaped leaves from desired decorative paper with decorative-edged scissors. Using craft brush, apply decoupage medium to one leaf. Lay down wire, then place second leaf on top, sandwiching wire between. Let dry, then bend into desired shape and wire onto heart.

6. Cut out images of birds, butterflies, bees, and flowers from nature-motif paper and decoupage to cardstock. Let dry, then cut out and hot-glue in place. Embellish with feathers, pearls, glitter, and ribbon.

7. Remove shoe insoles and set aside. Using foam brush, coat shoes with a layer of gesso. Set aside.

8. On a photocopier, lay out a piece of lace. Lay down the book print over the lace. Copy onto printer paper. Tear the paper into 1"-square pieces and decoupage onto exterior of shoes.

9. For the interior of the shoes, cut ½" x 1" strips from the decorative paper and decoupage on, starting at center back.

10. Trace shoe insoles onto decorative paper and cut them out. Decoupage the paper soles onto cardstock. Let dry, then cut out with decorative-edged scissors. Hot-glue onto insoles, then hot-glue insoles in place. Stuff shoe tips with excelsior.

11. To make adornments, copy lace onto printer paper. Decoupage to cardstock, then cut out in desired shapes.

12. Add some curves to the decoupaged shapes by bending the edges and tips. *Note: The best time to bend these pieces into shape is when they are not completely dry.* Hot-glue them onto the shoe as desired and embellish with a few pearls and rhinestones.

"One shoe can change your life."
—Cinderella

Andante Tap Shoes

The dancers mounted on these shoes were laser-copied from a black-and-white antique photo, circa 1920.

Accessories

½" foam brush
1" hole punch
Black paper
Cardstock
Colored pencils
Corsage pins
Craft scissors
Decorative-edged scissors
Decoupage medium
Hot-glue gun and glue sticks
Laser-copied black-and-white
   vintage photos of dancers
Old book print
Pair of tap shoes
Red crepe paper (2 yards)
Various decorative papers

1. Remove the insoles. Trace them onto decorative paper. Using craft brush and decoupage medium, decoupage onto cardstock. Let dry, then cut out with decorative-edged scissors.

2. Cut another sheet of same paper into several ½" x 1" strips. Decoupage onto interior of shoes. Let dry.

3. Hot-glue the insoles into the shoes.

4. Tear book print into 1" squares and decoupage onto exterior of the shoes.

5. Punch twenty-four dots from black paper. Decoupage over book print.

6. Fashion two big bows out of red crepe paper. Hot-glue bows across shoe straps.

7. Tint dancer photos with colored pencils. Decoupage onto cardstock. Cut out.

8. Hot-glue corsage pins to the backs of dancer photos. Mount the photos on shoes as desired.

Funky Clunkies

Enjoy embellishing a pair of wide-heeled shoes with paper tiles. The larger the heel, the more surface area to apply the tiles.

Accessories

Acrylic paints (optional)	Paper punches
Alcohol	(optional)
Cotton ball	Posterboard
Craft scissors or rotary	Sandpaper (optional)
cutter and grid	Spray adhesive
Decorative-edged	Stamps and ink pads
scissors (optional)	(optional)
Decoupage medium	Tacky craft glue
Lacquer	Variety of hand-painted
Masking tape	or purchased
Pair of wide-heeled	decorative papers
shoes with dense	Wallpaper knife
foam, cork, wood,	
or plastic heel	

1. Clean shoes with cotton ball and alcohol. If the heel is slippery (like plastic), sand lightly before proceeding.

2. Place masking tape around the area where tiles will be glued. *Note: This will protect the rest of the shoe from glue and finishing mediums.*

3. Glue decorative papers to posterboard with spray adhesive. *Note: This thickens the papers and makes them easier to work with. It also gives them dimension so that the final project will resemble mosaic. Use posterboard that is the same color as the shoe heels.*

4. Cut decorative papers into squares and rectangles, some as large as 1½".

5. Embellish some larger tiles as desired with paints, stamps, paper punches, and decorative scissors.

6. Glue tiles onto the heels of both shoes vertically and horizontally, using tacky craft glue. *Note: If a tile extends beyond the heel, you can trim it when the glue is dried. Paper tends*

to curl and move until the glue sets. *When papers lift, gently press them back into place until they stay down.* Let glue dry.

7. Carefully trim any tiles that extend past the heel edges with a wallpaper knife.

8. Cover the entire heel of both shoes in a thick coat of decoupage medium. Let dry.

9. Spray two coats of lacquer on the mosaic portions of the shoes, making sure the rest of the shoes are masked and protected.

10. Carefully remove masking tape.

11. If desired, add paper tile buttons. Create the tiles as in Steps 1–6, then coat them in decoupage medium and let dry. Seal with lacquer, poke holes, and stitch them on as you would a regular button.

Designer Tip:

Choose good-quality paper such as handmade, scrapbook, or gift wrap for paper tiles. Avoid construction or magazine papers.

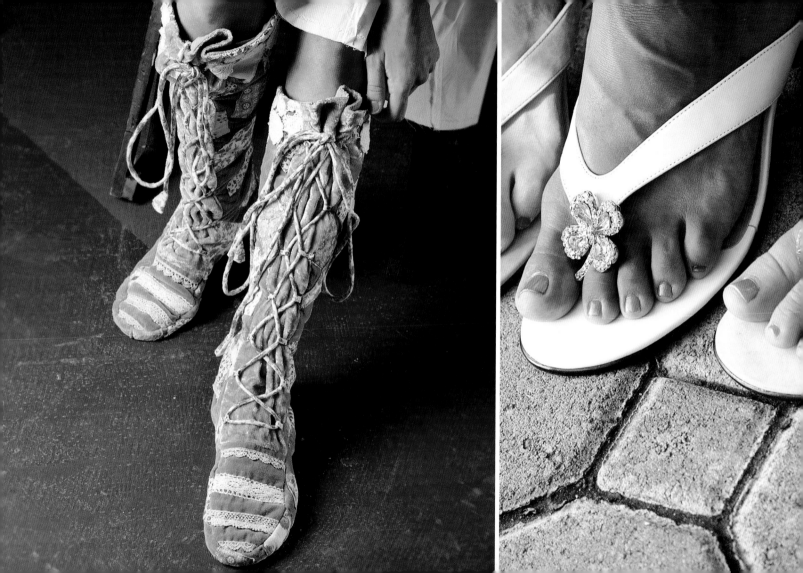

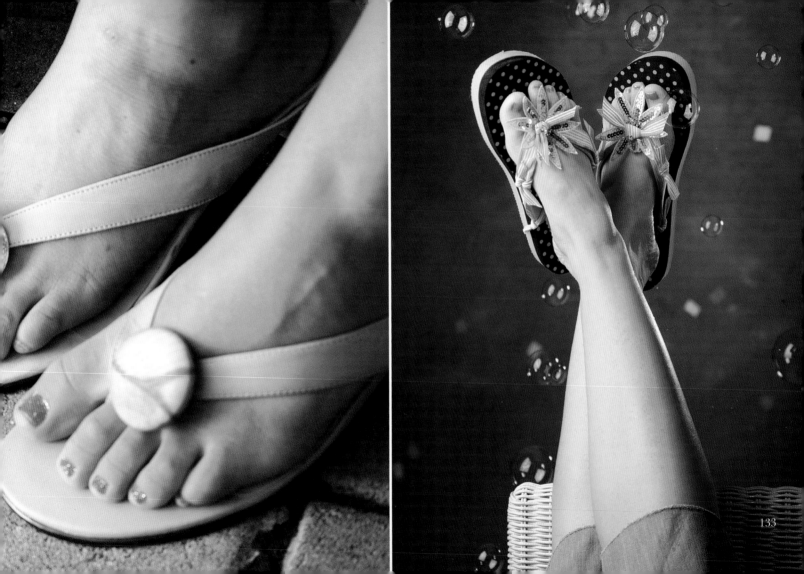

Patterns
Bright Toddler Slippers

Enlarge patterns 200%

Martini Party Shoes

Print patterns at 100%

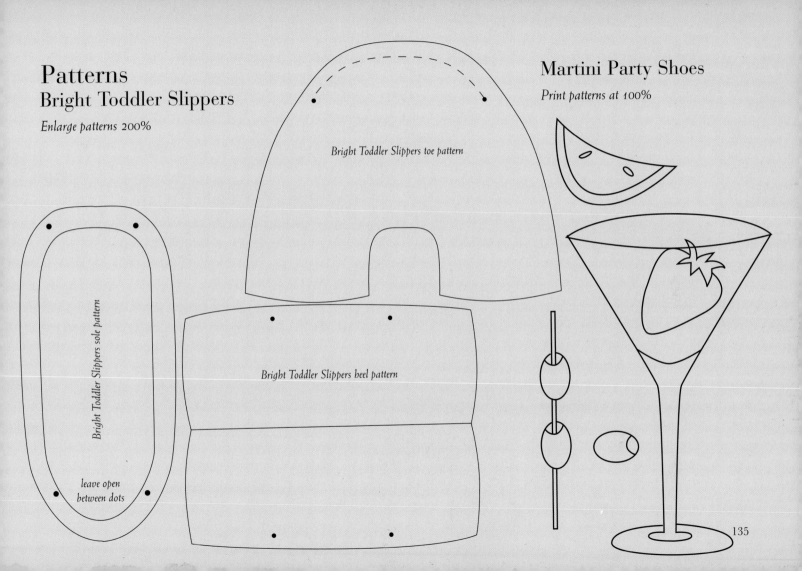

Bright Toddler Slippers toe pattern

Bright Toddler Slippers sole pattern

Bright Toddler Slippers heel pattern

leave open between dots

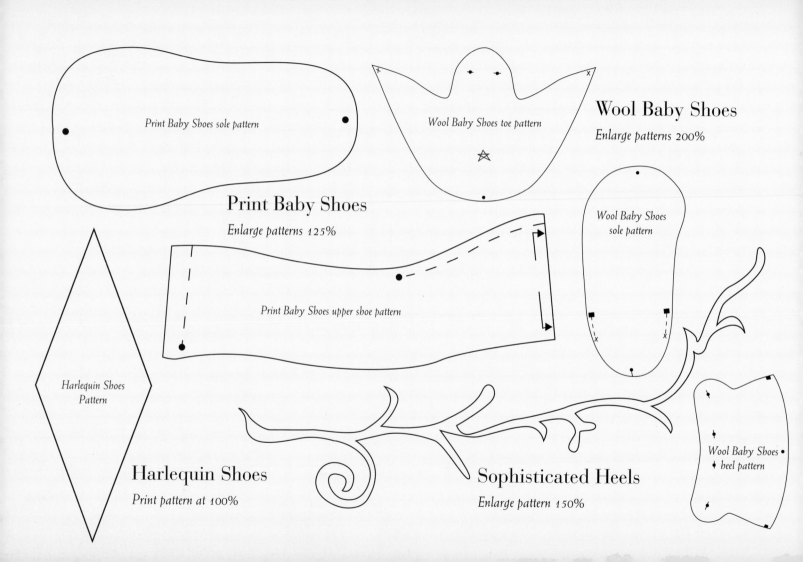

Print Baby Shoes sole pattern

Wool Baby Shoes toe pattern

Wool Baby Shoes

Enlarge patterns 200%

Wool Baby Shoes sole pattern

Print Baby Shoes

Enlarge patterns 125%

Print Baby Shoes upper shoe pattern

Harlequin Shoes Pattern

Wool Baby Shoes heel pattern

Harlequin Shoes

Print pattern at 100%

Sophisticated Heels

Enlarge pattern 150%

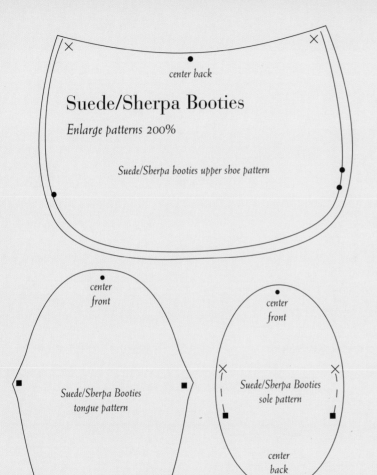

Suede/Sherpa Booties

Enlarge patterns 200%

Suede/Sherpa booties upper shoe pattern

center back

center front

Suede/Sherpa Booties tongue pattern

center front

Suede/Sherpa Booties sole pattern

center back

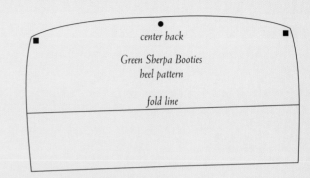

center back

Green Sherpa Booties heel pattern

fold line

Green Sherpa Booties

Enlarge patterns to 200%

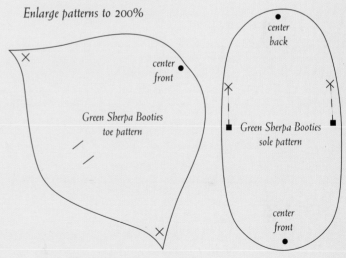

center front

Green Sherpa Booties toe pattern

center back

center front

Green Sherpa Booties sole pattern

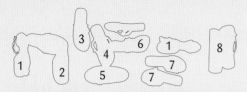  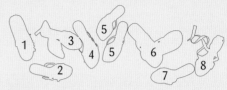

Put Your Feet Up (pages 16–17)

1. Hot-glue large silk flowers onto the toe. Hot-glue small flowers along the strap.

2. Slip-stitch beaded ribbon trim along the instep of a pink cashmere slipper.

3. Tie bows of various colors and widths along straps. Use a toothpick to place a dot of super-glue into the knot of the bow. Glue a rhinestone button or pin on the outside.

4. Havaianas Top, purchased as is.

5. Remove the center stamens of a flower pin and glue a glass bead onto each center. Pin or glue the flower in place.

6. Red Hatter Handmades, made for the Red Hat Society, purchased as is.

7. Glue glass beads onto the straps of slides, using industrial-strength adhesive.

8. Hot-glue two yellow flowers to the center post of the sandal strap. Cut off the shanks of two starfish buttons with wire cutters. Glue the buttons to the flower centers.

Stepping Out (pages 32–33)

1. Clip rhinestone earrings to black patent pumps at the toe.

2. Pin large rhinestone brooches around the strap at the open toe.

3. Glue glass beads onto heel and straps of chunky sandals, using industrial-strength adhesive.

4. Cut off a silk flower close to the stem. Glue to sandal strap with industrial-strength adhesive.

5. Adhere beaded trim to the underside of sandal straps with glue or double-sided adhesive sheets.

Walking Down the Aisle (pages 52–53)

1. Use industrial-strength adhesive to glue daisies onto white sneakers.

2. Use industrial-strength adhesive to glue floral trim along straps of sandals.

3. Use industrial-strength adhesive to glue a floral embellishment to toe of sandals.

4. Use industrial-strength adhesive to glue a length of jeweled trim along one sandal strap.

5. Use industrial-strength adhesive to glue a tiny flower to the cross strap of sandals.

6. Mossimo, purchased as is.

7. Use industrial-strength adhesive to glue a plastic flower to sequined sandals.

8. Adhere a length of white decorative braid to the strap, using double-sided adhesive sheets.

Running Around (pages 64–65)

1. Attach medallions to each shoe with clear glue, making sure that a portion of each medallion extends above the toe into the foot area.

2. Place each pin through the straps, positioning it so that it looks good on the shoes and the feet.

3. Karen Scott, purchased as is.

4. Glue silk flowers onto the toe of shoe.

5. Mossimo, purchased as is.

Walking Tall (pages 84–85)

1. Sew dangling bead trim along top edge of boot.

2. Use industrial-strength adhesive to glue a beaded feather embellishment to the outside of each boot.

3. Cut a feather boa to fit around the ankle of the boot, then sew the ends together. Repeat for the brim of the hat. Using brooch, pin up one side of the hat.

4. Tie wide ribbon into a bow around each boot, then adhere with industrial-strength adhesive.

Baby Steps (pages 94–95)

All shoes: Use industrial-strength adhesive or superglue to adhere flowers, bows, jeweled trim, buttons, or other embellishments to the toes of fabric baby shoes.

About the Authors

Jo Packham and Sara Toliver

Jo Packham is President of Chapelle, Ltd., a publishing company specializing in crafts and decorating books.

Her daughter, Sara Toliver, is Vice-President of Chapelle, and is the company's Marketing and Advertising Director. Sara and Jo also operate Ruby & Begonia, a gift and home decor establishment; The White Fig, a gift basket company; and Olive & Dahlia, a garden and floral boutique.

Participating in every corner of the craft world, Jo and Sara have used their creative expertise to found WomenCreate, an annual five-day symposium of more than 30 arts and crafts, held in Ogden, Utah.

Jo has authored several books, including *Decorate Rich* and *Extraordinary Touches for an Ordinary Day*. Sara is the author of *Vintage Christmas Crafts* and *Bountiful Baskets*. Together they are the authors of *Ruby & Begonia's Christmas Style*.

About the Designers

Karen Christensen

Shoes are shown on pages 16, 22, 24–25, 28, 70, 72.
A watercolor artist for 30 years, Karen Christensen has had works on display in private and government collections worldwide. In addition to designing prints, magazine illustrations, and logos for art fairs and businesses, she has designed a Christmas line for an East Coast marketing firm consisting of mugs, tins, paper goods, snow globes, and stocking hangers. Karen is married and has three sons.

Sue Ellen Cooper

Shoes are shown on pages 16, 130 (right).
The founder and Exalted Queen Mother of the Red Hat Society, Sue Ellen Cooper has spent time as a commercial artist, creating frameable prints and greeting cards,
and later starting a mural business. In July 2000, Sue Ellen founded the Red Hat Society. Since then, her artwork has appeared on the covers of *Red Hatter Matters*, the first official Red Hat Society publication. Sue Ellen lives in Fullerton, California, with her husband Allen.

April Cornell

Shoes are shown on page 132 (left).
For nearly 30 years, designer April Cornell and her husband Chris have beautifully translated her artful combinations of color and floral designs into exquisite collections of romantic clothing, linens, and home accessories. They also own a wholesale company and more than 110 boutiques in North America. She is the author of *April Cornell Decorating with Color* and *Designer Scrapbooks with April Cornell*.

Susan Cottrell

Shoes are shown on pages 16–17, 20–21, 23, 26–27, 29, 32–33, 36–37, 40–43, 48–49, 50–51, 53, 60, 62–63, 64–65, 66–67, 71, 73, 76–77, 82–83, 85, 88–93, 100, 131, 133.

Susan Cottrell studied art at the University of Utah and received a bachelor's degree in Drawing and Painting from Weber State University. Her studies were only the beginning of a life long education in the visual arts. Susan enjoys painting children's furniture, making quilts from paper and fabric, working with ceramics, and painting in watercolors and oils. She is surrounded by a very creative family and can imagine no other existence so wonderful.

Suzy Eaton

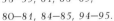

Shoes are shown on pages 30–31, 34–35, 44–45, 46–47, 52–53, 54–55, 56–57 (stockings), 58–59, 61, 68–69, 80–81, 84–85, 94–95.

Suzy Eaton realized her artistic abilities as a small child and has been mastering her technique ever since. She studied art at the University of Utah and at Weber State University. She has worked as a graphic designer, a photo stylist, and an artist, and her favorite medium is watercolor. She also enjoys furniture refinishing, remodeling, decorating, and mosaic work. Suzy resides in Ogden, Utah, with her three children Jordan, Danni, and Connor.

Sandra Evertson

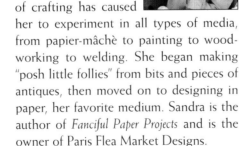

Shoes are shown on pages 106–115, 117–119, 121–125.

Sandra Evertson's love of crafting has caused her to experiment in all types of media, from papier-mâchè to painting to woodworking to welding. She began making "posh little follies" from bits and pieces of antiques, then moved on to designing in paper, her favorite medium. Sandra is the author of *Fanciful Paper Projects* and is the owner of Paris Flea Market Designs.

Mary Jo Hiney

Shoes are shown on pages 56–57 (shoes), 78–79, 96–99, 101, 102–105.

Mary Jo Hiney is one of the top fabric and ribbon designers in the industry. Her company, Mary Jo Hiney Designs, offers beautiful combinations of silk fabrics to quilt stores internationally. Hiney has been featured in segments on cable television programs, including HGTV's "Smart Solutions" and the "Carol Duvall Show," as well as Discovery Channel's "The Christopher Lowell Show." She has authored several books, including *The Beaded Object*, *Beautiful Foundation-Pieced Quilt Blocks*, *Creative Decorating with Ribbons*, and *Beautiful Quiltagami*.

Catherine Matthews-Scanlon

Shoes are shown on page 130 (left).

Catherine was born in Maine and has had a love for art and all things creative since her childhood years. When she left her Graphic/Web Design profession behind to become an SAHM, Catherine found she needed an outlet for her creativity, and that's when her passion for scrapbooking and creating altered items began. She currently works from home in Rhode Island as a freelance designer for EK Success.

Susan Seymour

Shoes are shown on pages 38–39, 128–129.

Susan Seymour made her first mosaic project from broken tile and was hooked, completing several projects before moving on to explore paper arts. She experimented with paper painting, collage, and papermaking before combining these with her love of mosaic. Now a full-time professional artist exhibiting and selling her artwork at festivals across the Southwest, susan is also the author of *Perfect Paper Mosaics*. She lives near Park City, Utah, with her husband and two children.

Marty Stevens-Heebner

Shoes are shown on pages 18–19, 74–75, 86–87.

After a friend helped her find her creative side, Marty Stevens-Heebner moved on to discover decoupage, decorative painting, and collage. Since then, she has been featured on HGTV and at arts festivals throughout Southern California. The inspirations for her work run the gamut, from frames decoupaged with safari photos to collages reminiscent of prehistoric cave paintings. Marty's company, Half the Sky, features her decoupage and jewelry designs and also offers in-home crafting parties.

Katie Stuart

Shoes are shown on pages 14–15, 17, 32–33, 127 (left), 134.

A graduate of the Art Institute of Chicago, Katie Stuart has been creating artglass for the past 15 years. Currently she focuses on lampwork, but also creates small fused beads used to embellish clothing, glass jewelry, and fused glass art. Katie has shown works at the Contemporary Arts Forum in Santa Barbara, California, has held numerous solo art shows throughout Boston, Massachusetts, and was the First and Second Place Winner in the glass category at the Fair and Expo 2000 in Santa Barbara.

Metric Equivalency Charts

inches to millimeters and centimeters

inches	mm	cm	inches	cm	inches	cm
1/8	3	0.3	9	22.9	30	76.2
1/4	6	0.6	10	25.4	31	78.7
1/2	13	1.3	12	30.5	33	83.8
5/8	16	1.6	13	33.0	34	86.4
3/4	19	1.9	14	35.6	35	88.9
7/8	22	2.2	15	38.1	36	91.4
1	25	2.5	16	40.6	37	94.0
1 1/4	32	3.2	17	43.2	38	96.5
1 1/2	38	3.8	18	45.7	39	99.1
1 3/4	44	4.4	19	48.3	40	101.6
2	51	5.1	20	50.8	41	104.1
2 1/2	64	6.4	21	53.3	42	106.7
3	76	7.6	22	55.9	43	109.2
3 1/2	89	8.9	23	58.4	44	111.8
4	102	10.2	24	61.0	45	114.3
4 1/2	114	11.4	25	63.5	46	116.8
5	127	12.7	26	66.0	47	119.4
6	152	15.2	27	68.6	48	121.9
7	178	17.8	28	71.1	49	124.5
8	203	20.3	29	73.7	50	127.0

yards to meters

yards	meters	yards	meters	yards	meters	yards	meters	yards	meters
1/8	0.11	2 1/8	1.94	4 1/8	3.77	6 1/8	5.60	8 1/8	7.43
1/8	0.11	2 1/8	1.94	4 1/8	3.77	6 1/8	5.60	8 1/8	7.43
1/4	0.23	2 1/4	2.06	4 1/4	3.89	6 1/4	5.72	8 1/4	7.54
3/8	0.34	2 3/8	2.17	4 3/8	4.00	6 3/8	5.83	8 3/8	7.66
1/2	0.46	2 1/2	2.29	4 1/2	4.11	6 1/2	5.94	8 1/2	7.77
5/8	0.57	2 5/8	2.40	4 5/8	4.23	6 5/8	6.06	8 5/8	7.89
3/4	0.69	2 3/4	2.51	4 3/4	4.34	6 3/4	6.17	8 3/4	8.00
7/8	0.80	2 7/8	2.63	4 7/8	4.46	6 7/8	6.29	8 7/8	8.12
1	0.91	3	2.74	5	4.57	7	6.40	9	8.23
1 1/8	1.03	3 1/8	2.86	5 1/8	4.69	7 1/8	6.52	9 1/8	8.34
1 1/4	1.14	3 1/4	2.97	5 1/4	4.80	7 1/4	6.63	9 1/4	8.46
1 3/8	1.26	3 3/8	3.09	5 3/8	4.91	7 3/8	6.74	9 3/8	8.57
1 1/2	1.37	3 1/2	3.20	5 1/2	5.03	7 1/2	6.86	9 1/2	8.69
1 5/8	1.49	3 5/8	3.31	5 5/8	5.14	7 5/8	6.97	9 5/8	8.80
1 3/4	1.60	3 3/4	3.43	5 3/4	5.26	7 3/4	7.09	9 3/4	8.92
1 7/8	1.71	3 7/8	3.54	5 7/8	5.37	7 7/8	7.20	9 7/8	9.03
2	1.83	4	3.66	6	5.49	8	7.32	10	9.14

Index

Andante Tap Shoes 124–125
Appliqué 13
Baby Mouse Booties 110–111
Baby Steps 94–105
Beach Stompers 22
Bead Dangle Boots and Hat 90
Beaded Animal Stripe Boots 89
Beaded Floral Sandals 63
Beaded Fringe Flip-flops 27
Beads and Buttons 14
Berry Terry Flip-flops 26
Blossom Sandals and Hat 40
Braided Rope Mules 37
Bright Toddler Slippers 96–97
Button Pumps 58
Chapter Opener Instructions . . . 138–139
Clay Roses Shoes 59
Coil Braid Flats 73
"Cute as a Button" Boots . . . 92–93
Dangling Bead Moccasins 76
Dotted Shoes 80–81
Exotic Asian Heels 36
Fancy Footwork 106–134
Feathered Mules 42
Flashy Foil Strappies 38–39
Floral Butterfly Shoes 69
Floral Trim Wedding Shoes 61

French Knot Slippers 28
Funky Clunkies 128–129
Girly Decoupage Shoes 30–31
Glass Beads 14–15
Glitzy Sequined Heels 49
Grapevine Sling-backs 41
Green Sherpa Booties 101
Harlequin Jester Shoes 46–47
Have Passport, Will Travel
    Sneakers 74–75
Heirloom Boots 86–87
In-love Doves Wedding Shoes . 114–115
Introduction 8–9
Jacquard Heels 78–79
Jeweled Ballet Slippers 43
Jewelry 13
Lacy Floral Shoes and Stockings . 56–57
Leopard Toe Flats 77
Luxe Quilted Slippers 29
Martini Party Shoes 44–45
Metallic Ribbon Sandals 48
Metric Equivalency Charts 143
Paint 12–13
Patterns 135–137
Peacock Mules 34–35
Persimmon Froglette's
    Toe Shoes 108–109
Polka Dot Flip-flops 24–25
Polka Dot Shoes and Purse . . . 68

Pretty Pink Moccasins 71
Puffy Paint Sneakers 100
Put Your Feet Up 16–31
Rhinestone Buckle Boots 91
Rhinestone Sneakers 23
Ribbon Canopy Sandals 50–51
Ribbon Flats and Hat 62
Ribbon Toe Mules 66–67
Ribbons and Trim 12
Running Around 64–83
Silk Flowers 12
Sophisticated Heels 54–55
Spotted Boots and Hat 88
Stars and Stripes Pumps . . . 82–83
Stepping Out 32–51
Suede Flats 70
Suede/Sherpa Booties 104–105
Tips and Ideas for
    Decorating Shoes 10–15
Top Dog Sneakers 18–19
Vintage Print Baby Shoes . . . 98–99
Walking Down the Aisle 52–63
Walking Tall 84–93
White Roses Mules 60
Wooden Bead Moccasins 72
Wool Baby Shoes 102–103
Woven Ribbon Flip-flops 20–21